Content Area
Literature Circles

Using Discussion for Learning Across the Curriculum

Content Area Literature Circles

Using Discussion for Learning Across the Curriculum

Holly Johnson

Lauren Freedman

Christopher-Gordon Publishers, Inc.
Norwood, Massachusetts

Copyright Acknowledgments

Christopher~Gordon Publishers, Inc.
Bridging Theory and Practice

1502 Providence Highway, Suite #12
Norwood, Massachusetts 02062
800-934-8322
781-762-5577
www.Christopher-Gordon.com

Printed in the United State of America
10 9 8 7 6 5 4 3 2 1   07 06 05

ISBN: 1-929024-84-3
Library of Congress Catalogue Number: 2004110625

Contents

Acknowledgments

This project could not have been completed without the help of teachers in West Texas and Western Michigan who believed that middle level students should voice their connections, concerns, and interests through content area literature circles.

Holly would specifically like to acknowledge and thank the 17 students who participated in the Spring 2002 EDLL 6344 course at Texas Tech University whose experiences with content area literature circles provided the basis for further research and her contribution to this text. Those women are: Holly B., Shelly E., Kimberly G., Cherryl G., Alison H., Jennine H., Jennifer M., Kathryn M., Amy P., Rosemary P., Keeli P., Lori P., Phyllis P., Autumn R., Amanda R., Vicki S., and Regina W. Examples of how their students performed in CALCs as well as their own thoughts about CALCs litter this text. They are still teaching and still providing space for CALCs in their classrooms even as high stakes testing looms above. They are truly inspiring!

Introduction

The northeast United States is a storehouse of the nation's history. When traveling through the region, tourists and residents alike are confronted by national memory and personal curiosity. What happened when the Pilgrims landed? How did people live? What relationships did the Indians have with the earliest settlers? When did the colonists really decide to attempt independence? What is the significance of Ellis Island? The Statue of Liberty? The Empire State Building?

Lauren experienced some of these questions one summer when she traveled to the Northeast with her grandson Trevor. They were visiting Lauren's sister Penelope in Boston and decided to get in one last sight before ending their vacation in the Northeast. All three expressed interest in visiting New York City, specifically the Statue of Liberty. They targeted a weekend in mid-July to tour the statue, and added Ellis Island, the Empire State Building, and the United Nations to their itinerary.

As they rode the train from Boston, they talked about various means of traveling, distances, and the concept of metropolitan areas. On the boat trip to the Statue of Liberty, they discussed how boats were made, how boats float, and how many passengers could fit into the one on which they sailed. They wondered about immigrants coming into New York Harbor and how the people—in fact, their relatives—could see Lady Liberty just as they were seeing her that day. Interested in the size of the statue and the pale green coloring, Lauren mused on the history of the statue and how she came to stand on that particular location.

As they waited in line to go up into the statue, Lauren and her family's interest heightened. Wondering about the construction, the architect, and the statue's height, Lauren, with a fervent, "I can't stand it any longer!", marched into the gift shop and purchased a book about the statue and its history. The book contained the facts she sought, but also information she hadn't. As Lauren read, she shared with the other two. "Listen to this! Did you know that the statue was designed by the same architect who built the Eiffel Tower?" She also shared that the statue came in pieces and how it was assembled.

As Penelope and Trevor asked more questions, Lauren passed the book to them. Each read and shared their thoughts and interests. They looked through the index for information, asked questions about the meaning of the inscription on the statue, and continued to tell each other their discoveries of the island, the statue, and its history. They also shared their connections to other ideas, historical sites, and architectural structures. They found that while many of their interactions revolved around what they were experiencing that day, at other times their discussion included the prior information each of them had, which helped them to make sense of what they were learning.

As Lauren shared her vacation with Holly, we came to realize that her time with Penelope and Trevor was filled with stories elicited by one of the most popular tourist sites in the nation. Lauren's story of her trip to the Northeast showed how often the two of us discussed our interests in history with each other, and how our interests in history produced stories about ourselves and our connections to our nation's past as well as to information about other nations. We also realized that our conversations and stories did not stop with history. They also revolved around Holly's interest in nature—trees, beavers and dams, wolves in Yellowstone—as well as around our mutual interest in geography. Questions of distance, typology, and environment are ever present in our thinking about the world and in our conversations. Those questions often result from an incident—a story—that allows us to use our mathematical and geographical knowledge. Our stories not only help us clarify our knowledge and beliefs, they also contextualize what we know so we can more easily share with one another and, by doing so, add to it.

As teachers and learners, we realize that when we talk with one another we do not limit our conversations to one particular topic or one specific way of thinking about the world. We share facts and theories, connections to our lives and to the outside world. We ask questions and attempt solutions; we ponder aspects of the world that confound us, and we express delight in the ways in which we use language for humor, analogy, chronology, perspective. We laugh; we defend our opinions and concede other ideas when convinced of their validity. In essence, when we talk we share ourselves, the information we know and have learned, and the ideas we hold.

It is from our thinking about our own dialogues that we have come to believe that students should be given the same opportunities within their content area classrooms. They should be able to tell their stories and the stories of history, geography, science, and mathematics. We have also come to believe that content area literature circles will invite young people to think about the world, all that there might be to know about it, and how they connect with it. It is with these ideas in mind that we developed this book and the learning strategies it contains.

Outline

We begin in chapter 1 by exploring the definition of content area literature circles (CALCs), their benefits, and their structure. We address how CALCs can be either text driven or concept driven, depending on a teacher's purpose. We also share an example of a CALC as it unfolded in a sixth-grade science classroom. This example shows how CALCs can create the kind of free-flowing discussion that supports students' knowledge acquisition while also producing an enjoyable way of learning.

In chapter 2, we discuss the steps we used to implement CALCs into middle school classrooms. These steps provide teachers with the process they might use to teach their students the routines for smoothly entering and sustaining a CALC. We offer suggestions for scheduling, planning, and preparing students for rich discussions. We also offer ways to troubleshoot some of the management issues teachers may encounter.

Chapter 3 deals with the types of materials that will enhance both the level of discussion and the amount of learning achieved through CALCs. We discuss the value of quality trade materials and address ways in which you will be able to enhance your students' use of a variety of text structures and genres. We also offer selection guidelines so that all students will have the opportunity to engage with both print materials and their classmates regardless of individual reading levels.

Chapter 4 begins a series of three chapters that focuses on specific strategies for engaging students in a CALC. Through the use of strategies that initiate discussions from their readings of information-laden trade books and textbooks, students learn how to identify and discuss the key ideas of the materials they read. They can also learn to think in ways that connect the information to their own lives.

In chapter 5, we present strategies that address the specialized vocabulary found in content areas. Through these CALC strategies, students can begin to build a solid basis for content knowledge acquisition.

Chapter 6 addresses strategies to help middle school students understand and appreciate other points of view or the multiple perspectives from which any problem or solution can be viewed. Students come to look more closely at how a text gives authority to certain perspectives, which may need to be questioned.

Chapter 7 highlights the importance of question and problem posing along with critical literacy skills. Students often have difficulty creating questions to think critically about author intent and bias in the text. Through strategies that can be used in CALCs to encourage questioning, students can become more critically literate. In addition, middle level students find it difficult to recognize problems, another critical thinking skill that can be developed with their peers in CALCs.

In chapter 8, we explore various strategies to assess CALCs. We address the purpose of assessment, the differences between formative and summative assessments, and particular types of assessments that are beneficial for continuous student learning.

In chapter 9, we present plans for CALCs across the academic year. We share an example lesson plan utilizing a CALC in one 48-minute class period from Ms. Mueller's sixth-grade classroom. We then present how CALCs are used in one of Ms. Mueller's social studies units, and finally, we share how Ms. Mueller plans to use CALCs across the academic year.

Throughout the book, we present excerpts from CALCs with real middle-level students. We also offer instructional activities for you to use to demonstrate to the class, learning activities for your students to try in their own small groups. Throughout the text we also emphasize the importance of reflection and self-evaluation for both students and teachers.

CALCs address both the social and the academic needs of the students while maintaining the curriculum. Because students identify comprehension difficulties and expand their understandings of texts, CALCs help readers to become more literate, more articulate about content knowledge, and better critical thinkers (Robertson & Rane-Szostak, 1996; Short, Harste, & Burke, 1996). Working with other teachers in Texas and Michigan as they learned how to use CALCs with their own middle-level students, we have watched students become more involved in and excited about their content studies. We invite you to use CALCs to incorporate rich, student-led discussions in your classrooms. We know that these discussions will enable your students to stretch toward deeper, more independent content learning and reading comprehension.

Chapter 1

Literature Circles in the Content Areas: What They Are and Why They Work

The most powerful and pervasive way that humans communicate with one another is through their connections and stories. Just think about it. How often do you tell a story to explain yourself, your ideas, or just to let someone know what you've been through in a day? How often do you watch television shows or movies that tell a story, either real or imaginary? It's human nature to communicate through stories, regardless of our context. Story is the glue that holds our ideas together and allows us to communicate our ideas to others in a recognizable format.

Once we started to think about how often we tell stories, we realized it was time for us to accommodate our students' stories—not only in language arts, but in math, science, social studies, music, and the other related arts. We found that when we allowed students time to include the necessary components of a story, they were better able to access their prior knowledge and make connections to what they were learning. We found that it is

We All Tell Stories

Is it difficult to believe that people talk mostly through stories or narrative form? Try an experiment. Listen to those around you talk. Listen as they respond to their life's experiences and their ideas about them through personal connections and personal metaphors and through bridging analogies created from their own experiences.

Try another experiment. Attempt to banish story from your communications with others for only one day. Most likely, you will find it impossible. As human beings, we want to share our stories about—and our connections to—the events and people that participate in and help create our lives.

through our stories and the stories of others that we can bridge the gaps between what we know and what we might learn.

Content Area Literature Circles

As the students pour into her fifth-grade science classroom, Ms. Richards is not surprised that they bring their stories with them.

> Daily, I am bombarded with what they have thought about, read about, or experienced while we have been away from each other. This is a kind of energy that I want to make use of so they will learn what I have prepared for them each day. In order to do that, we do a lot of talking.

Comprehension and Content Area Learning

Reading comprehension of content textbooks involves more than the words on the page and their pronunciation. Textbooks frequently include graphs, figures, and illustrations that can help readers understand the written text more fully, yet middle school students can have difficulty with understanding that type of information. Sometimes students can pronounce the words but do not understand their meaning or how they are being used. At other times, particular content areas will use words differently and/or with different meanings. Students need to understand how language works in specific content areas so they can comprehend what they are reading. By discussing how language is used, how particular content areas view and use information, and how meaning may be different in math, science, social studies, and language arts, students can create schemas or frameworks for the various content acquisition.

Talking is important to the social as well as the cognitive development of early adolescents. Because it is something they have already incorporated into their daily lives, it just makes sense to use it in an academic setting as well. That is why Ms. Richards makes use of talk as one of the primary ways her students learn. They do a lot of their talking in content area literature circles (CALCs), where they share stories and build knowledge together about the content under study.

Ms. Richards' fifth graders are also learning that as people proceed through their daily lives, they "story" (Freedman, 1996) with each other. That is, they tell stories together, each adding a piece to the story with a comment, a question, an addition, an example, a connection. This phenomenon is a result of our social nature as human beings, yet too often it is not used in content area classrooms. Theodore Sarbin (1986) asserts that "human beings think in narrative structures, they make meaning through the use of [stories]" (cited in Cooper, 1995, p. 123). If our students are to make the deep and lasting connections with content knowledge that we want them to, they must make this knowledge their own.

One of the best ways to accomplish this is through discussions that enable them to transform the content information into stories they tell each other. Through discussion, students enrich content knowledge by making meaningful links between what they are learning and their lives. Students take science, social studies, and mathematics information and create stories of science, social studies, and mathematics that they can more readily and easily integrate into meaningful, usable, memorable "folders" in their minds. Their stories and the content knowledge we want them to learn can be accommodated in CALCs. CALCs provide students with the opportunity to integrate the content information they have been reading in their print materials (trade books or textbooks) and explore it in multiple ways. CALCs also address comprehension issues that often plague middle school content teachers.

The Definition of Content Area Literature Circles

Content area literature circles (CALCs) are student-led, small-group discussions built around a particular book or concept. They are different from typical classroom discussions where the questions at the end of a chapter or textbook selection become the focus of the interaction (see Table 1-1). Because CALCs are student-led conversations, students make connections to their lives and to other content that they don't often have the opportunity to make. Through collaboration with peers, each student's comprehension of the material is also much stronger, and the content concepts and supporting details are more easily learned.

Table 1-1.   Content Area Literature Circles and Other Class Discussion Strategies

CALC	Other Discussion Strategies
Similarities	
Students talk.	
Students ask and answer questions.	
Students share information from texts read.	
Differences	
CALC	**Other Discussion Strategies**
Student-led discussion	Teacher-led discussion
Students take turns speaking.	Students are called on by teacher.
More voices are voluntarily heard.	Limited number of voices are heard.
Students generate the questions and the answers.	Teacher provides questions and answers students' questions.
Students use facts and details to support their ideas.	Students recite facts and details to demonstrate knowledge.

CALCs are based on literature circles, a dialogue-based activity used most often with narrative texts that allow students to discuss a particular text in small groups (Daniels, 2002; Peterson & Eeds, 1990). CALCs proceed in ways similar to literature circles in that they support students' learning while addressing the teacher's desire for students to demonstrate and apply their learning in relation to the curriculum (see Table 1-2). In CALCs, however, students typically discuss informational texts with an expository text structure or narrative texts with a focus on nonfiction content. CALCs are distinguished from other forms of group work by the blending of an efferent (academic) purpose with an aesthetic (emotional) engagement (Rosenblatt, 1978).

Table 1-2.   Content Area Literature Circles and Other Literature Circles

Content Area Literature Circles	Other Literature Circles
Expository or informational texts	Narrative or poetic texts
Concepts, content, subject focus	Literary focus
Efferent purpose with aesthetic response	Aesthetic purpose with efferent response
Assessment focused on knowledge and application	Assessment focused on response and reflection

The process of CALCs is frequently the same as with typical literature circles. They provide a "forum in which students have opportunities to discuss and share interpretations and understandings of a text" (Flint, Campbell, & Halderman, 1999, p. 7). In the case of CALCs, those texts are informational in nature and often expository in structure. We believe that the information about science, social studies, or mathematics should be open to student interpretation and critique; thus CALCs allow for such higher order thinking skills.

Another parallel to literature circles is that students often decide what to discuss based upon their own interests and the information they have read. In many literature circles in language arts classes, however, students focus on one common reading. CALCs are used in the acquisition of content knowledge and understandings in science, math, and social studies, and frequently center on multiple materials. Although most middle-level students are familiar with reading and discussing narrative texts, the experience of reading nonfiction or expository texts with a view toward discussing the information and ideas is new to many of them. CALCs are a great way for students to practice and use strategies that help them comprehend information and informational texts.

The Place of Content Area Literature Circles in the Classroom

Finding a place for content area literature circles (CALCs) may seem like an overwhelming task for teachers who are unfamiliar with how they work. In Figure 1-1, we have produced an instructional model that illustrates how CALCs work within content classrooms. This visual representation presents the power of organized, structured talk within a classroom environment. Since talk is an essential learning tool and CALCs provide students with a framework on which to "hang" their talk, CALCs serve as an integral part of the work of the classroom. Used for a multitude of purposes within various units of study, CALCs easily accompany all of the other language and literacy strategies—reading, writing, thinking. The kinds of talk vary from connections to self to persuasion to problem posing to generalizations. As all of the strategies and engagements surrounding the three circles suggest, CALCs can be used to strengthen the learning impact of these strategies when used as an introductory activity, within the engagement, or as a follow-up. Examples are given below.

As a way of introducing a unit, the students might browse through a text set of multiple materials and then share their impressions within their CALC groups. As the teacher familiarizes the students with the prompts (to be discussed in chapter 2) for beginning and sustaining discussions, she might have the students choose the one they think will generate the most input from each of their members. Students might choose to share ideas, issues, or attributes. They might choose to share questions, connections, significant language, what they have learned, or why the information is important. It is also possible for the students to move easily within and among these prompts as their discussions continue.

As middle-level students are working on preparing a readers' theatre, they might engage in a CALC to discuss the information they need to include, making sure of its accuracy and relevance for their fellow classmates, their audience. They accomplish this through peer leadership, turn taking, ensuring that all voices are heard, generating pertinent questions, and deriving reasonable answers that have sufficient support based on information and reason.

Another example might involve a CALC following a teacher read-aloud. During the CALC, the students gain increased accessibility to the ideas in the reading, motivation to continue with the exploration of these ideas, comprehension support, connections that support lasting learning, critical thinking, ownership of their learning, support for English language learners, practice with both efferent and aesthetic stances, and support to practice democracy.

Figure 1-1. Content Area Literature Circles: Part of a Learning-Centered Classroom

CALCs may appear on the surface to be only a single instructional strategy, yet they provide such a wealth of possibilities for student learning that they can be used again and again. Although the basic premise for them remains the same, when they are well facilitated and guided, students use them for many different learning purposes, thus making each CALC a fresh experience.

Even though CALCs offer a wealth of possibilities, they remain one learning tool among many available to middle school teachers and their students. Regardless of the instructional focus, CALCs serve as a complement to the variety of instructional strategies used in math, science, social studies, language arts, and the related arts to promote content knowledge and conceptual understandings.

The Three Phases of Content Area Literature Circles

Content area literature circles (CALCs) can involve three stages or phases of discussions. In Table 1-3, we briefly describe these phases and what kinds of talk happen when middle-level students discuss their readings, their connections, and their new learnings with each other. We have found that most discussions progress along these lines when students are familiar with discussion and are given the time to proceed through these stages. Although we want our students to be involved in all three phases, we know that sometimes this is just not possible. Depending upon the time allotted during the day, the week, or the unit, teachers can schedule one phase of CALCs or all three, building the depth of the discussion over a series of days.

Table 1-3.　A Series of Three CALCs to Discuss Content

First Literature Circle
"Dinner Table Talk":
Sharing of ideas; clearing up misconceptions; general talk about content under study
Second Literature Circle
Issues or Concept Discussion:
Selecting particular issues connected to content and "going deeper"
or
discussion of a central concept
Third Literature Circle
Process Discussion or Further Issues and Concepts:
Students reflect on their process of discussion, work accomplished, group dynamics
or
continue with another issue or concept related to the topic

Initiating the Discussion

When we first enter a discussion with others, especially if we have not worked with them in the past, we typically start by trying to get a common understanding about what the others know or think. In discussing a particular concept or text, we check for similar understandings, or if we are confused about something, we ask others to help us clarify what we didn't comprehend. In first encounters with others, we don't often get into the deeper issues right away, but rather play along the surface until we are sure of each other and of what the issue, content, or problem involves. In CALCs, we often call this "dinner table talk" (Atwell, 1998), because like the dinners we experienced as young people, our conversations were often superficial, with each member reporting about their day or asking general types of questions. Deeper issues were not addressed until after dinner. First discussions in a small group often revolve around superficial topics or ideas, with the deeper issues and engagements planned for later. Because our students often stay at the surface in their first conversations with each other, we plan for the first CALCs to last approximately 20 minutes. At the end of this discussion, students then generate a list of deeper issues, ideas, or problems they can address in their next CALC.

Engaging the Deeper Issues and Concepts

The next time our students meet in CALCs, they focus on the list of issues, ideas, or problems they generated at the end of their first discussion. This is also the time when we ask students to attend more closely to the content materials they read prior to their meeting so they can share actual quotes, pictures, or content from that material. We suggest that this is when real dialogue begins, with students sharing their connections to the materials, their judgments of the content or issue, and their passion or lack of it with each other. Because they have met with each other previously, they are more comfortable with each other and thus have fewer difficulties sharing what they are thinking.

When students meet the second time and engage more deeply with the content, we know that planning a particular time length is more problematic. We have watched sixth graders engage each other and content material for 45 minutes without any prompting from us. We also know, however, that when middle-level students are first learning to work in CALCs, they may feel less comfortable with the process. Thus, we plan for this second level of CALCs to last about 20–25 minutes. At the end of their time together in this literature circle, students can decide to meet again to discuss other ideas or issues they did not address or they can move to the third stage of CALCs by reflecting upon the process. Often this decision must be made with the teacher, who knows more about the curricular demands of the classroom.

Reflecting on the Process

The third phase of a CALC is the stage where students reflect upon the process they have just gone through as a small discussion group. During this literature circle, students reflect upon what they have learned and how they have learned it. Typically, students evaluate the strategies they learned or used to help with content acquisition, they ponder how others in their group were especially helpful with their learning, and they also evaluate how they participated with others. This is when students also think about what strategies didn't work or where they didn't perform as well as they could. We don't often ask students to evaluate others in negative terms, but by hearing or reading what our students say about others in a positive manner, we can indirectly gauge how well particular groups of students worked together.

Lasting about 25 minutes, these CALCs are beneficial for middle-level students because otherwise students don't often reflect upon their learning processes. By talking about their discussion and learning processes, middle-level students come to better understand how they learn and what strategies they use well and can employ for future learning.

The Types of Content Area Literature Circles

We find that content area literature circles (CALCs) fall under two types, depending upon the materials the teacher selects and the purposes of the discussion. By understanding the strengths of the two different types of CALCs, teachers can plan CALCs that will help their students benefit from their discussions not only personally but academically. Each serves a useful purpose for student learning; thus it is up to teachers to decide which type of CALC they wish their students to pursue. "Antonio, a Negro," one of the sample stories in the next section, is used a number of times throughout this book to illustrate various attributes of CALCs. We repeat the use of this example because we find that using familiar material can allow teachers who are unfamiliar with CALCs to focus on our description of how they can be used rather than on the example itself.

Concept-Driven CALCs

Concept-driven CALCs revolve around a topic, theme, or content concept rather than one particular text. Students read or view a variety of materials prior to meeting in their literature groups and then discuss that topic, theme, or concept, rather than a particular text that could contain information across a wider spectrum than the specific topic under study. These literature circles are more focused than text-driven CALCs because the students are more intent upon making connections to the concept rather than the multiple connections they could make to one text. For instance, if students are discussing war as a concept, they will make closer connections to that concept and may use particular wars as examples of the concept. Because their focus is on the concept, they will also make comparisons that are appropriate. If they are reading a particular text about the Civil War, however, they can make connections to particular battles, the conditions of the soldiers, the communities and families at home, the letters people wrote, the food eaten, and so forth. Their focus is wider but no less appropriate for learning. In the following example, four fifth-grade students discuss the rain forest after reading several short texts that their teacher, Ms. Richards, checked out of the library.

Annalisa: *What did you think was interesting in your book?*

Tómas: *Stuff about the kinds of animals that live in the different parts of the rain forest, like in the canopy and stuff.*

Peter: *You mean, like sloths? Can you believe anything is that slow?*

Delores: *I'm about that slow when I gotta go to the dentist. I hate going to the dentist. I would rather just go down the Amazon River.*

Tómas: *You worry too much about the dentist. What about the rain forest?*

Delores: *I liked the part I read about the jaguars. They aren't seen very often, but wouldn't that be cool to see one?*

Annalisa: *I wonder if there are any in the San Diego Zoo. We're supposed to go visit my brother in California, and we are going to the zoo when we go.*

Peter: *Hey! What's that area called, like, called, like a bio, a bio, what's that word?*

Annalisa: *You mean a biome?*

Peter: *Yeah, that's it. I found out that there are more kinds of things in a tropical rain forest than in any other biome. That's probably why they are so important and people get mad about cutting down the trees.*

Tómas: *How much kind of stuff is in a biome?*

Peter: *I read that 50% of all living things in the world live in a tropical rain forest. Up in the canopy and on the floor, and that one other part.*

Annalisa: *The understory!*

Tómas: *Did you read that part about the frogs? Man, I never seen so many different kinds of frogs and, and what they do! Some of them can probably kill you.*

Peter: *But, but, the part about how many different kinds of things live in the rain forest—they live in only, like, 2% of the world.*

Delores: *If I went to the rain forest, I would want to study the different kinds of plants. My book had all kinds of stuff about plants in it. Some people say the plants are used for medicines all over the world.*

Annalisa: *I would want to see the different kinds of monkeys that live in the trees. I think orangutans live there, and other kinds of smaller monkeys.*

Peter: *Primates!*

Annalisa: *Are monkeys primates?*

Delores: *I think we might have to look that up 'cause I don't know that at all.*

This CALC on the rain forest shows that while students told stories from their lives, they remain focused on biomes and the rain forest in particular. The depth of comprehension of the information is evident in their conversation. The connections they are making contain the quality of ownership not usually found in content classrooms.

Text-Driven CALCs

The second type of CALC that we use with middle-level students is text driven. Students read a common text (typically informational or expository) before they meet in their literature circles, and then they discuss the content of that text and how it connects to their lives. These discussions are beneficial for middle-level students' initial encounters with a topic because they allow students to cast a wide net in terms of connections and experiences. If we want our students to think about a topic, period, or situation in a general sense, we often find one book that addresses that interest or content, and then we allow our students to concentrate on making that content accessible to them. In the following example, four sixth-grade students from Ms. Mueller's social studies class engaged in a CALC after they read an excerpt from the book *Building a New Land: African Americans in Colonial America* (Haskins & Benson, 2001). It was during the second week of a unit on social justice, and the students were familiar with CALCs. This was their initial CALC on the text.

Bernabe: *He won his freedom, right? Did his wife? How does that happen, anyway?*

Julianna: *Yeah, and how does he get his own farm? Did he still work for the Bennett family when everyone moved? Do you think his wife might still be a slave to the Bennetts?*

Nick: *I don't understand why people had to get permission to marry each other.*

Vanessa: *That's probably because slaves weren't treated like people, but like property.*

Julianna: *How could people think that way?*

Bernabe: *Prejudice! Some people still think that way about Blacks and about Hispanics, too.*

Vanessa: *What kind of plantation do you think it was?*

Nick: *It says there's cotton and I think they probably had some other crops.*

Bernabe: *Where's the Jamestown Colony and the Chesapeake Bay? Are they in Virginia? The person who wrote this thinks we know all this stuff!*

Julianna: *Well, why don't we? We learned it last year!*

Nick: *Yeah, but who remembers? I don't even know where Virginia is now.*

Vanessa: *Did you read the part where Antonio, or Anthony, I guess he changed his name. I wonder why he did that? But anyway, did you read where his farm burned? He got his taxes reduced to rebuild. I want to know how did his farm burn? Do you think it was prejudice? But then, who reduced his taxes? How did that work?*

Bernabe: *Yeah, for all the trouble he probably had being Black, it's amazing that White people reduced his taxes when they could have just said, "Tough luck, dude."*

Julianna: *I think someone probably helped his farm burn, but other people weren't prejudiced and helped him out later.*

Nick: *Later in the story, it talks about how he lost some tobacco—hey! Maybe the plantation grew tobacco! But he lost some tobacco and the courts didn't do anything to help him and he didn't help himself. Why didn't he do anything?*

Vanessa: *Well, it says the times were changing and White people were taking advantage of free Blacks. Why would people do that?*

Bernabe: *Prejudice! I mean, they even took his land from his family after he died because he was an alien. What's that supposed to mean? Like he was from outer space or something?*

Julianna: *No! It's like Mexicans who come over the border. They're called illegal aliens. They aren't from here. But if that was true, how did Antonio get over here?*

Vanessa: *Slavery. I don't understand how White people can bring other kinds of people over here and then say they don't belong here.*

Julianna: *It isn't just the White people. Antonio or Anthony, whatever, he had slaves, too! Why would he do that? How did he treat them, I wonder?*

Nick: *All of this stuff doesn't make any sense to me. It's like those people back then didn't think or something.*

This CALC shows how students can discuss many aspects of a common reading. Because these four students had different interests and saw different things in the same text, they were able to help the others gain information they would have missed by reading and writing independently. They expanded their understandings of the material they read while also addressing some of the issues that were only hinted at in the text.

The Benefits of Content Area Literature Circles

The reasons to use content area literature circles (CALCs) are multiple and varied. They provide students with the opportunity to engage with one another in authentic dialogues, help students to learn in real ways, and also provide an appropriate venue for students to learn content. Specifically, CALCs have the following benefits that can produce more willing and passionate learners.

Make Content More Accessible

Often textbooks are not compatible with students' reading levels, which can be frustrating to students and teachers alike. Content area literature circles (CALCs) do not depend on the members of the circle reading the same text, watching the same movie, or hearing the same speaker. Students can read or view a variety of materials and bring that information to a discussion. Or, if reading a common text, students can fill in the gaps that their group members did not grasp in the reading, which can benefit teachers who do have specific content that they want their students to learn (see chapter 2 for more information about teacher purposes and CALCs). By asking students to fill in the gaps of their peers' understandings, we do not mean that only the better readers help those challenged by a particular text. Often we have seen students who have difficulty reading bring another perspective or additional insight to the discussion after they have listened to their peers talk about an idea, concept, or issue. Students use all types of information and experiences to gain understanding about the content, and they use different learning styles to access the information they gain from CALCs.

For example, Ms. Richards' students learn in a variety of ways. John is an interpersonal learner. He likes to talk and does well when he is able to comment on the information he is learning. Discussion works well for him. Tim prefers to read and write about what he is learning. Discussion can be problematic for him. Lindsay likes to demonstrate her learning. Her kinesthetic approach was often a struggle because she was expected to stay seated and quiet in most of her classes. In a CALC, however, these students' strengths can be used initially to engage them and then, through the social interaction with their peers, help them to develop additional learning strengths. Students might begin their learning based on their areas of strength, but when they come to CALCs, they are able to teach each other how to use alternative strategies for learning and sharing their content knowledge.

Engage and Motivate Students

Through discussions in content area literature circles (CALCs), students' voices, questions, concerns, ideas, and intellectual lives become an essential element in the curriculum, which increases their active participation in their own learning (Johnston, 1992). In reality, adolescents love to talk. They want to share with their peers, their parents, and their teachers. A striking paradox is that although young people love to talk with one another and their teachers about any number of things, when asked to engage in the recitation of facts from a textbook or lecture information in their content classrooms, many students become silent. In many classroom interactions, the fear of being wrong or of looking stupid is a powerful deterrent to participation. Another factor contributing to their silence is that although young adolescents usually want to tell their stories, talking in front of large numbers of their peers is not an experience they relish (Barnes & Todd, 1995).

Given the opportunity to talk with others about the ideas and concepts required of them in their content classrooms in ways that interest and relate to them, young adolescents will open up and share what they know. CALCs as a part of their learning motivate students to share and analyze information with others in relevant, interesting, and engaging ways. We also found that students bridge knowledge from one topic to another with an incident from their lives. By adding such details to the discussion, students learn who has a deep interest in the topic and could more readily explain it in language they can understand, which builds interest about the topic in others. In CALCs, students help each other to remember the information they found interesting, thus increasing the entire group's engagement of the topic.

Build Comprehension

James Wertsch (1981) suggests that peer-directed discussions are less rigid than the adult-child interactions that frequently take place in school. When students talk to one another, there is a common bond of adolescent culture (Kaiser, 1994), which allows students to communicate in ways that may be more understandable to some of them than the talk of their teachers or the textbooks frequently used. Because students can bridge information for each other and can bridge the barriers often established in adult-child interactions in which students may feel inhibited about telling the teacher they don't understand the information, more learning takes place.

Kathy Short, Jerome Harste, & Carolyn Burke (1996) assert that through the conversations and dialogues within literature circles, "readers have the opportunity to explore their half-formed ideas, to expand their understandings through hearing others' interpretations, and to become critical and inquiring thinkers" (p. 479). Students are able to explore their "rough draft understandings" (Short & Pierce, 1990) in conversations where the focus is on the attempt to understand the information found within a text. In content areas such as science, social studies, and mathematics, learning is based on theories and ideas as often as factual information already proven. Teaching students to theorize and evaluate information helps them to build their knowledge of the content subject. Through content area literature circles, students connect this knowledge to themselves, their lives, the world, and other texts, thus improving their comprehension skills (Keene & Zimmerman, 1997).

Advance Lasting Learning

By making connections within and between content areas, students also build their motivation to know. They make passionate connections to topics that may last a lifetime. Ian, a sixth grader who didn't particularly like science, found that by talking about marine life he has now "become obsessed with marine biology. That's what I want to learn about and study in college." Also interested in writing, he suggested that he "could write about what I learn about sea turtles. They are my favorite marine life." At 11, Ian has a plan that was created through free-flowing talk about mammals.

Another lasting benefit of content area literature circles involves students' abilities to remember the knowledge they have learned and to make that knowledge relevant to their own lives and interests. By creating their own stories and bridging the knowledge from their own lives with information in their content classrooms, students learn more and remember the subject information they are asked to learn in school. They also learn how important and relevant the knowledge they do learn in school can be to their personal lives.

Enhance Critical Thinking

Often young people do not realize that even "the facts" do not include all the information that they need to understand fully the situations or conditions people face in their lives. Textbooks often give facts that privilege certain understandings and certain peoples. We find that middle school students can question the content in terms of who or what is left in and who or what is left out; thus they develop critical literacy skills that help them to determine the authenticity and accuracy of the texts that they are reading.

By allowing students to discuss issues of authority, or the issue of who gets to write or say what within the texts they use to learn content knowledge, teachers demonstrate not only how knowledge changes but also how knowledge is situated to present information in ways that may not be beneficial for all peoples. For instance, presenting westward expansion and Manifest Destiny without looking at the displacement of American Indians allows the myth of progress as a positive movement for all peoples to persist. In content area literature circles (CALCs), students ask questions about who did not benefit from such progress, which allows them to wrestle with alternative perspectives on historical, scientific, and mathematical "advancements." They can also ask questions about authors' purposes or intentions for writing about a certain subject, idea, situation, or event in the way that they did. Students can also discuss what the author might want to share about a particular topic or incident as well as what the author might have overlooked or forgotten to address. With critical literacy skills gained in CALCs, middle-level students can also address the concepts of *fact, opinion,* and *bias.* In CALCs that encourage students to view information from multiple perspectives, students begin to develop a broader and deeper understanding of the content studied.

Encourage Students' Sense of Ownership

In content area literature circles (CALCs), students are involved and exhibit various degrees of background knowledge and personal connection. They show areas of interest and are ready to ask questions of each other and theorize about what they are learning. In CALCs, students share information that mirrors what they already know, supports what they already think, challenges and corrects their misunderstandings, and provides new knowledge that expands what they know and understand. In essence, CALCs are an integral part of allowing students to own the knowledge they share with others. We see how important talk is to adolescents, and by utilizing this energy in our classrooms, we can create learning spaces where students bring their questions, comments, and connections to the topic under exploration. By working with students' natural propensity for sharing through talk, we create learning environments "where students search for meaning, appreciate uncertainty, and inquire responsibly" (Brooks & Brooks, 1993, p. v).

Support English Language Learners

Discussion gives English language learners the opportunity to learn the academic vocabulary that they often don't readily grasp when attempting to learn both the language and the content found in their textbooks. Through content area literature circles, students are able to work through their interpretations, their misunderstandings, and what they wish to know in more focused and involved ways. Also, students working in literature circles are more able to scaffold other students' knowledge by making analogies that are relevant to their worlds; other student members support each other's learning in very real and concrete ways. Through their reading and discussion, students who are learning English are expanding their vocabularies, trying on new ways to talk about their learning, and experimenting with the language they are learning in academic contexts.

Allow for Both Efferent and Aesthetic Stances

Too often in content area reading, we ask students to read simply to extract information. Although gleaning facts and key ideas is important, it does not make for eager, satisfying reading. When we allow students to engage with the text in meaningful ways, however, the facts and ideas become more relevant to them and therefore more accessible. Using literature circles as a tool for discussing informational texts in the content areas allows students to explore the texts from both aesthetic and efferent stances (see Table 1-4).

Table 1-4. Efferent & Aesthetic Purposes for Reading

Efferent	Aesthetic
Focused on information gathered during the reading	Focused on "lived through" experience gained during the reading
Reader's concern will result from the reading	Reader's concern happens during the reading
Disengaged from personal feelings and elements found through reading	Engaged with broader feelings and meanings

Because an efferent stance emphasizes readers concentrating on what information or concepts will "be left when the reading is over" (Rosenblatt, 1978, p. 27), content area literature circles (CALCs) are especially useful for the content areas. Students voice what they have read and understood, and they listen to others' learning as well. With a more aesthetic reading, the attention is consciously focused on what the words are stirring up "during the reading event" and the feelings that such information gives them.

CALCs allow students to focus on the more aesthetic exploration of content knowledge, thus giving them the opportunity to make emotional connections to the information while also finding pleasure and deeper meaning in their discoveries. Learners who involve themselves emotionally as well as intellectually in their work gain greater comprehension (Frager, 1993).

Support Democratic Classrooms

Richard Ruiz (1991) asserts that by allowing student voice to become part of the curriculum, not only do marginalized students become more active participants in their classrooms, but "the discussion of themes with other students demonstrates how one's individual voice can be joined with other voices to effect social action on behalf of the community" (p. 224). Essentially, using discussion allows all students to be heard, and all students to speak, thus enabling more democratic practices between all those within the classroom.

Content area literature circles are a natural aspect of such learning environments because they are dialogues in which learners communicate about the content under discussion with an attitude of "reciprocity." They share their ideas and new understandings with one another as equal and valid members who have something important to share with the others.

The Theoretical Underpinning of Content Area Literature Circles

The use of content area literature circles (CALCs) revolves around the social construction of knowledge. Based on the concept of constructivism, "individuals bring past experiences and beliefs, as well as their cultural histories and world views, into the process of learning" (Lambert, 1995, p. xi). Thus, CALCs allow students to build knowledge from their own experiences with print in connection to others' ideas of the textual information. Working together to interpret what they have read, students deepen their knowledge of the content under study as well as learn how their personal knowledge is expanded by discussing their ideas with others.

Social construction of knowledge facilitates the development of a community of learners, where "both individual and collective growth are valued, as are the processes for achieving that growth" (Walker & Lambert, 1995, p. 15). Students bring to the classroom their experience and understandings about the world. In CALCs these understandings are brought to the forefront of the conversation, where students can build on or reshape the knowledge they already possess, or they can reconstruct misconceptions that need to be changed. Together students learn about the content under study, but they also learn about themselves and each other, creating a community in which all learners come to rely upon the experiences and knowledge of others as well as themselves. They also learn that the world is socially constructed, which allows them to understand the diverse ways in which their peers know and come to know the world. This allows for diversity in learning and being.

John Dewey (1916) espoused that learning was a social experience and that young people should have authentic experiences at school to facilitate their own understandings of the world and their roles in it. His philosophy of learning was inquiry based, in which students could ask their own questions about the content they were learning. In CALCs, students are free to inquire about the content within a context that is safe for them to do so. They do not risk their uncertainty in front of large groups.

Lev Vygotsky (1978) views individual learning as being influenced by a social context. Students learn through their connections to others who have spoken about, written about, or thought about the ideas they study. Walker and Lambert (1995) suggest that "learners build their interpretations of the world through engagement with their culture and their peers, through engagement with big ideas, and by recognizing and forming new patterns. In the process, they self-construct themselves as learners" (p. 26). CALCs facilitate young people's awareness of the social nature of learning and of themselves as learners who are constantly reinterpreting and reflecting on what they study. They can also apply this knowledge in meaningful ways with others.

Conclusion

Using content area literature circles (CALCs) in middle-level classrooms brings together student lives and subject area content in an interactive process that benefits the entire learning community. Ralph Peterson and Mary Ann Eeds (1990) assert that when young people read texts, they create their own interpretations that "vary with experiences, attitudes, personal literary histories, and purposes . . . [and] when interpretations are shared with a community of readers, different people's interpretations enhance the potential for making meaning for all" (p. 16).

By writing this book, we want to share the enthusiasm we have witnessed in young adolescents as they venture out to theorize about the world and their role as citizens within it. As with most strategies for learning, the results will not necessarily be the same across all classrooms, or even all content literature discussions in the same class. As teachers become more familiar with how CALCs work with their students, they will make changes that fit their classrooms. The use of discussion for understanding content, however, cannot be overstated when it comes to working with and learning from middle-level students.

Chapter 2

Preparing for Content Area Literature Circles

> *At first I didn't quite know how to work with content area literature circles in my class. But once I tapped into the students' natural curiosity about some of the information they were learning in their other content classes, I decided that those interests could be facilitated in my reading and writing workshop. I am excited by what my students have to say.*
>
> —Victoria Saunders, eighth-grade language arts and social studies teacher

Ms. Saunders believes that her language arts class is a place where any kind of content knowledge can be discussed. "When my students come in from science discussing body parts and organ transplants, I make connections to Frankenstein and experimentation. They see the bridge established between two supposedly different content areas." As she realized the need to accommodate her students' questions and interests, Ms. Saunders saw a connection between the literature circles her students used to discuss short stories, poetry, and novels and the value of discussion for learning social studies, the other content class she taught in her middle school.

As she continued to think about ways to use literature circles in her social studies class, Ms. Saunders also began utilizing more of the content knowledge her students were learning in math and science to connect with the topics she addressed. This way her students also read and discussed primates, diabetes, and geometry in her class, thus making more authentic connections to all that they were learning. In middle schools where teaming is in place, using content area literature circles becomes a way to integrate content. Ms. Saunders' dilemma, however, was establishing and maintaining real discussion that would engage her students as they learned about all the things that interested them.

Planning for Content Area Literature Circles

Learning how to plan for content area literature circles (CALCs) is a first step toward creating real discussions in math, science, and social studies. Learning to think about ways to use literature circles in language arts classrooms when we ask our students to read biographies and other informational texts was also a dilemma we faced when we first thought about informational texts, content learning, and connections to the language arts. We also wanted to utilize discussion as a way of bridging content knowledge when working on interdisciplinary units. What we discovered is that teachers can easily use content area literature circles as a way to bring seemingly unrelated content concepts together so that students can see how these concepts fit together, but learning how to dialogue requires planning in terms of students, materials, and time.

In this chapter, we discuss the logistical considerations that teachers need to address when using CALCs in their curriculum. We found that addressing and planning around these elements makes for more productive and pleasurable CALCs. We discuss teacher planning that addresses preparing students for discussion, student grouping, selection of materials, the purposes for discussion, scheduling, assessment, and the use of teacher read-alouds to acquaint students with discussion and response to informational texts. We discuss these elements in the sequence in which we plan for our own classrooms. Thus, we discuss the idea of how to introduce CALCs to our students. Table 2-1 lists the necessary elements.

Table 2-1.   Elements to Consider When Addressing CALCs With Students

---

- Students' Familiarity With Discussion

   Do students understand the difference among *discussion, conversation, lecture,* and *reporting*?

- Strategy Teaching and Learning

   Are the students familiar with the strategies that initiate discussion or the prediscussion strategies to prepare for discussion?

- Students' Ability to Self-Govern in Small Groups

   Have students met in small groups before? Are they familiar with the expectations for behavior in small groups?

- Small-Group Sharing

   Do students know how to share in small groups so that each person has the opportunity to talk?

- Negotiation of Purpose, Process, and Productivity

   Have the students had the opportunity to help develop curricular expectations?

Preparing for Classroom Discussions

One way to begin thinking about using content area literature circles (CALCs) is through discussion itself. If students are familiar with a classroom organization that depends on students working together, then they are more apt to understand and feel comfortable with discussion. If students are expected to work more independently, they will most likely need more time and guidance in adapting to sharing their ideas and stories with others. We suggest, however, that at the beginning of the school year, few middle-grade students are adept at discussion; thus, we would always plan to prepare our students for literature circles by using whole-group discussions to address issues of turn taking, reader response, and levels of discussion.

   When we ask our students to discuss anything in the classroom, we frequently find that they want to talk only to the teacher rather than to each other. To facilitate opportunities for students to talk to one another, we would read aloud an informational picture book such as *A Picture Book of Sojourner Truth* (Adler, 1994) or *Faithful Elephants* (Tsuchiya, 1988), which address issues that evoke an emotional response in students. We then ask a general question, such as "What do you think?" or "What connections can you make to this?" Once we asked a question, however, we "move over" to allow students to talk to one another rather than to us. As in most classrooms, this is a difficult first move for both teachers and students. Thus, we facilitate this student-to-student relationship by asking our students to talk to specific people across the room while, we assure them, we are listening. This often produces giggles or awkwardness when discussions are introduced, but as we continued the practice our students began to rely on us less and less as facilitators of discussion. At other times we avoid direct eye contact with the students so they will seek another face to address. We explain to our students why we do this and add that we are always listening, but that they need to talk to others in the classroom community, too.

Popcorn Strategy for Learning Turn Taking

In a random, popcorn fashion, students take turns counting aloud up to the number that corresponds with the number of students in the group without planning the way they will begin to count around the room. Each student may only call out one number in the sequence.

The catch comes when two or more students say the same number at the same time. The counting has to begin again, but in another direction. Students learn that they must pay attention to others, to the body language of others, and to others' facial expressions so they will know when they can speak.

This activity requires that students watch others, and that is the most important part of turn taking—considering others in the group.

In the adjoining sidebar, we share one strategy addressing turn taking that was given to us by a colleague who found that middle-level students especially enjoy the activity. The benefit of the strategy is that the students learn the importance of watching body language and facial expressions while also taking into account the verbal pauses and speaking styles of others.

We typically spend the first month of school introducing CALCs and practicing discussion in whole-group dialogues. We teach mini-lessons on the flow of discussion, moving from one level to another (see chapter 1), and the purpose of discussion. Once students are comfortable with discussion, we move to selecting smaller groups for discussion, saving whole-group discussions for later in the year, when we plan to use whole-group discussions to address particular strategies that we want our students to learn and ways to gauge their own participation in discussions. These later discussions are planned according to our particular purposes, goals, or outcomes.

Selecting Small Groups for Content Area Literature Circles

The benefits of content area literature circles (CALCs) are multiple and varied. Yet they do not come without their own set of issues. Some of these involve classroom challenges such as student participation, group construction, and small-group interactions. How to form and maintain the literature circle groups is an ongoing process. The purpose of the literature circle should govern both the number of students within the group and the demographics of the group, because there are times that teachers will want to limit either the size or the particular student makeup of the groups.

Self-Selected Groups

Thinking about personalities must be a consideration when planning CALCs. We find that students naturally gravitate toward those who think like them or who are their friends. We allow self-selected groups when students are first learning to talk to one another in small groups as well as when we have figured out which particular combinations of students will work well together. When first introducing CALCs, we find that students will more readily talk to one another if they are familiar with one another, thus increasing their comfort level and familiarity with literature circles. As the year goes on, we negotiate with our students about grouping so that all students will benefit from the community of learners. Once student groups begin to work efficiently with the same group members, we allow for longer periods of self-selection.

Long-Standing Groups

It is often most valuable to have long-standing groups so that the students get to know each other well and develop trust with one another. These long-standing groups work best when there is diversity among the members, both academically and socioculturally. The growth of trust will allow students to take risks in their learning that they might not take with other members of the community with whom they are not as familiar. The depth of learning that can be created from long-standing groups that function as a learning community cannot be underestimated. Again, we do negotiate changing long-standing groups throughout the year so that students have the opportunity to talk with others in the classroom.

Jigsaw Groups

Once long-standing groups have been established, it can be useful to reform groups for a particular purpose. This type of grouping would allow students to hear different perspectives on one particular aspect of a text, an issue, or a content subject. Students in the long-standing group might each choose to become part of a different group working on a common text. They would then have the benefit of sharing the information gathered in the multiple-copy groups with their long-standing group. For example, temporary groups could form around specific shorter texts or articles. In a study on planets, groups could be formed around planet books by Seymour Simon—*Saturn* (1985), *Mars* (1987), *Mercury* (1992), *Neptune* (1997), *Jupiter* (1998), *Venus* (1999). After the reading and discussion, each member of these temporary groups would rejoin his or her long-standing group to share the information and ideas.

How teachers decide to group their students often depends on what they wish to accomplish in their class as well as the personalities involved. We have grouped students in a variety of ways, and we are still not convinced that one way works best for all students, classrooms, or teachers.

Choosing What to Cover

In this section, we discuss two major considerations that teachers need to take into account when preparing students for content area literature circles (CALCs). The first is determining the students' prior knowledge. The second issue concerns finding materials to use in CALCs. These two elements may be the most critical for the success of CALCs.

Determining Students' Prior Knowledge

One of the first considerations when thinking about preparing students for content area literature circles (CALCs) is to determine their schemata for the study at hand. *Schema* (pl., *schemata*) refers to people's organization of information from their experiences into patterns that make sense to them. The information is interrelated and often overlaps with other patterns the mind has created. As we learn, we continue to add or reshape the information into more and more meaningful patterns that can become more specific or more inclusive of other concepts and ideas.

For example, when you go to a restaurant, you may not know what to do with all the silverware on the table, but when you go to a fast food restaurant you will know what to do because of your past experiences with restaurants. When you go to a new city, you have some ideas about how cities work, with one-way streets and stoplights. However, you do not know where certain streets or points of interest are because you have not visited this city before.

When our students read, they also refer to past experiences with particular words, concepts, or textual structures. That is their schemata at work. They are accessing the meaningful patterns they have created about particular aspects of reading. For example, when thinking of the color red, they might refer to the rainbow, their favorite bicycle, the color wheel, or the idea of anger or passion. As they continue to build a schema about red, students may develop patterns based on objects or on color theory, science experiments, or flags of countries. A schema for particular information may connect specifically with one content area, and students may have a difficult time understanding its meaning in another context. Therefore, preparing your students for accessing appropriate schemata or building new patterns for connecting information is important as students enter a CALC.

In the following excerpt from a literature circle in Ms. Mueller's social studies class, we can see how students who don't have an appropriate schema for the information might become confused about the topic. With CALCs, however, students can address their misunderstandings that might be due to inappropriate schemata or lack of prior knowledge. The excerpt shows how students can guide each other in relation to correcting misunderstandings brought about from lack of prior knowledge about the content. Ms. Mueller read aloud the picture book *Elsie's War: A Story of Courage in Nazi Germany* (Smith, 2003) and then asked the students to discuss what they had learned from the passage. One student has a difficult time with the whole concept of the Holocaust, but as the questions and conversation proceed, we see that all of the students have difficulty with the concept of time and when the Holocaust occurred.

Betio: *When did this happen?*

Alicia: *During World War II, when the Nazis did all those terrible things to the Jews.*

Betio: *Why did people let that happen? I mean, why didn't we do anything about it?*

George: *We did! We went and defeated the Nazis.*

Betio: *I don't get it, though. When was that war the book is talking about?*

George: *A pretty long time ago, like way before we were born.*

Alicia: *Do you think Ms. Mueller was born then?*

Betio: *Let's ask her!*

Ms. Mueller is called over to the discussion, and on hearing the question, laughs. "That was before I was born, too." She hands the book to Alicia. "Take a look at the book and think about the dates included in it. Then decide where it would fit on our timeline of the world." Ms. Mueller leaves the group to address other issues in other literature circles.

Alicia: *It starts right here with 1933, and then on the next page it says "After the war began in 1939—"*

Betio: *Are there any other dates in there?*

George: *Here's another one. It says, "At last, in March 1945," and it talks about how American soldiers came.*

Betio: *That's a long time for a war to last. So, when was it, in comparison to us? I was born in 1991. When were you born, George?*

George: *1990. What about you, Alicia?*

Alicia: *In July 1991. Wow!—1933 was a long time ago! Did they have computers then?*

Betio: *Or computer games?!*

George: *Or refrigerators? Electricity, even?*

Betio: *I'm gonna ask my grandpa if he was living then.*

Alicia: *He might not have—let's go put these dates on the timeline.*

This passages shows that young people can have difficulty with concepts of time. Ms. Mueller finds that this is a major issue when teaching history to her sixth-grade students. It is from overhearing this kind of misunderstanding about time through CALCs that Ms. Mueller now addresses her students' prior knowledge about time before embarking on the unit.

Finding Materials for Content Area Literature Circles

Although chapter 3 provides a full discussion of the selection of texts, we thought it would be useful to offer a few ideas about the text selection here as it is an important consideration in using content area literature circles (CALCs) to their fullest potential. To make content accessible for CALCs, you will need to consider the following when selecting texts for your students to read and discuss:

- Use materials that cross a variety of reading levels.
- Use materials with photographs, graphs, figures, and other visuals.
- Use texts that present diverse perspectives.

In addition to determining what materials to make available for students to read and discuss, you will need to determine how to familiarize your students with what you are making available to them.

One example of this is Mr. Robine's seventh-grade science class's study of the solar system. Mr. Robine briefly shared through book talks the texts he had selected for his students to use. He then invited his students to use the books within the classroom to find information that related to the questions they were most interested in discussing. The elements of a book talk are as follows:

- Read part of the prose.
- Show the connection to the content.
- Engage the students through questions that the text might answer.
- Display visuals that students will find of interest.
- Name the title and the author.
- Create suspense, if appropriate.

Students scurried all over the room choosing books that seemed interesting. As they opened the books, Mr. Robine noticed that the students were most interested in studying the photographs and illustrations in their books. They then began to read the written text to find out more. After 20 minutes, Mr. Robine asked his students to gather in their CALC groups. For the rest of the 50-minute period, the students engaged in CALCs about the solar system. They shared their questions in their small groups first, and then they began to discuss the information they found that might answer those questions. Mr. Robine's one criterion for these CALCs was that the students make certain that they took turns sharing and asking each other questions so that everyone could contribute.

After the discussion, Mr. Robine noticed how the students eagerly shared with one another the answers to some of their questions. What surprised him, however, was how his students expanded their discussion beyond simply answering their own and each other's questions. They made personal connections to the information they shared, generated more questions that deepened their understandings of the solar system, and then began to speculate about the universe and how the world's understanding of it would change in the future. They made intertextual connections to *Star Trek* adventures and the science fiction they read during free reading. They recommended particular titles to other students who had not read any science fiction, and they gently teased those who hadn't seen a *Star Wars* movie. They wondered what it would be like to be astronauts and if there was actually life in other galaxies. As they talked, Mr. Robine noticed how they became more excited about the concepts of black holes, wormholes, meteor showers, and the northern lights. He also noticed how often they borrowed books from other groups to increase their content knowledge. It was through Mr. Robine's use of a variety of materials across reading levels that allowed all of his students to learn and share information with the rest of the classroom community.

Determining the Purpose for Discussion

As with all good planning, it is necessary to know the purposes, goals, or outcomes for each content area literature circle (CALC) in relation to your students' learning of all of the following aspects of a CALC: content, collaboration, discussion, and themselves as learners. If students do not create meaning for themselves about what they have read or learned, then their participation in content subjects is wasted. At the middle level, this is a concern many teachers express. They often wonder if their students are learning anything. With CALCs, teachers can ascertain what their students are learning and not learning by listening to them as they talk or by recording them on audiocassette recorders for reviewing after school. The following set of questions can be helpful in setting purposes, goals, and outcomes:

- What content do I expect my students to acquire?
- How can I utilize student interest?
- What prompts can I give my students that will facilitate the discussion?
- At what points in the unit will discussion be valuable?

One of the earliest challenges that Ms. Saunders faced when attempting a CALC for the first time was determining the expectations she had for her students. She wanted them to enjoy their small-group discussions, but she also wanted them to accomplish several academic goals. She hovered over a number of her students as they talked, which made them self-conscious and nervous. Because of her worry, the students did not make the connections she later realized they could have made.

Some of the teachers we worked with wondered how using CALCs would address the content they were teaching. Because they felt they had so much to cover in 1 week or one marking period, they were concerned that the students wouldn't learn what they wanted them to learn. As these same teachers incorporated CALCs into their plans, using the prompts and strategies that we suggest go along with particular learning objectives, they found that their students did learn the content and made deeper connections than they had anticipated.

Addressing the curricular mandates is a challenge that all teachers face, but CALCs do not neglect the content or the curriculum. We see them as providing avenues for students and teachers to meet the learning outcomes in ways that bring students into more active participation with the content material. We have also found that some content cannot be addressed well in CALCs. Using CALCs is one way of student learning; lectures, labs, and individual projects are others. Together these approaches keep the content lively and allow for all types of learning and learning styles. The following are prompts that we found especially engaging for middle-level learners:

- What ideas, issues, or attributes do we notice in this material?

- What questions can we make or pose concerning this material?

- What connections can we make to other content, to our lives, to the world?

- What significant words, phrases, or passages are of special interest to us?

- What have we learned?

- Why is this information important to us, to the world, to the content area?

Planning for CALCs begins with a combination of elements: curricular standards and benchmarks, the district curriculum, the student's interests, and the classroom context. We recommend that teachers decide the purpose of the CALC by reviewing the curriculum framework for the course and then determining when they would like their students to engage in discussion. One way Ms. Saunders works with CALCs is by having different prompts for talking in CALCs posted on a bulletin board in her classroom. This way the students can automatically refer to the list, as well as be reminded of what they might focus on if Ms. Saunders doesn't have them focus on a particular way of thinking for that day.

By working through demonstrations and prompts, Ms. Saunders' students were able to work in CALCs that focused on a number of different ways to read content material. She also wanted them to learn different strategies that would help them to answer the larger questions.

It often works best when teachers and students negotiate the purpose of the CALC, as this allows students more opportunities to make personal connections. Students at the middle level need "a wide range of strategies to comprehend, interpret, evaluate, and appreciate texts" (Wilhelm, 1996) as well as access to additional materials. Thus, strategies and practices that allow adolescents to use the various language arts are especially useful for acquiring content area knowledge. By planning CALCs, teachers can always use a variety of strategies to complement the CALCs while addressing students' various needs and learning styles.

Your students, with guidance from you, can determine how CALCs should work in your classroom. For instance, working with a group of seventh-grade students on a study of the solar system, we asked them what information would be most relevant for them to know. After brainstorming what they thought would be important, we asked their teacher, Mr. Robine, what other information he would add to cover the curricular mandates of his state and district. "Interestingly enough," he commented, "the students have already listed everything they would need to know to be prepared for any test I would want to give them." This is not to say that the students already knew the information, but they knew the general categories that Mr. Robine might wish for them to know when they were finished with their study of the solar system. See Table 2-2 for their list and the additions from Mr. Robine.

Table 2-2.   Concept Generation for a Study of Space

Concepts Generated by Students	Concepts Added by Mr. Robine
Distances	Names of all the planets
What planets are made of	Which planets have moons
What the sun is made of	Definition of space
How it was all created	
How big they are	
Stuff about meteors and comets	
Gravity	
Orbits	

The teachers we work with have their students first use the materials they've just read by discussing the information on a surface level. Questions to ask themselves and to share with others revolved around what they thought about the information, how it connected to their lives, and what parts of the reading they didn't understand. This first discussion allowed all members to speak and to clarify any misinformation or misunderstandings about the content. As the year went on and students became more familiar with CALCs, we encouraged students to deepen this superficial discussion of the material by asking them to pose problems from the material, create analogies or bridges from one concept to another, create comparisons and contrasts to other material they have read, and reflect upon how the reading did or did not engage them. These types of discussions created the promise of more in-depth understanding of the content.

Valuing social and cultural connections with content concepts is another way to make students feel comfortable about their own content connections. Often students don't make direct connections between their life experiences and content concepts, or they make connections that at first might appear to be inappropriate. It is important for us as teachers to get underneath these experiences and connections and make use of them to help students grasp the concepts. For example, during a study of machines in Mr. Dornan's eighth-grade science class, Rodney kept talking about carnival rides. Rodney did not think of himself as a good student or a good reader, but he was willing to give ideas that interested him a chance. So when he started to make a connection between certain aspects of simple machines with the carnival rides he loved, Mr. Dornan saw an opening to suggest that he look in *The New Way Things Work* (MacCauley, 1998) for details and connections to the concepts of levers and pulleys that he had been talking about in their study of simple machines.

Determining How Materials Will Be Read

There are a number of ways to share print materials in the classroom. The following three ways lend themselves especially well to content area literature circles (CALCs).

Teacher Read-Alouds

This is useful particularly at the beginning of a unit, for the introduction of new concepts within a unit, or for the first time CALCs are used. The advantage of using a teacher read-aloud is that all of the students in the class share a common text from which to initiate their discussion. It allows you to focus the discussion and use it as a demonstration if that is one of your purposes. It also allows students to access more easily a more complex text and gives you an opportunity to examine the terminology and make direct connections with students' lives.

Common Text

Each of the four to six members of a CALC reads the same text. This could also be the same text for all the groups, or there could be choices so that each group is reading a text different from the other groups. The advantages of this common reading are that it allows for a common focus, for students to share understandings and confusions, and for them to develop questions that they will have about the material. This gives you increased insight into the concepts that you will need to focus on instructionally. A caution for this choice is that all students need to be able to read the common text, so it should be one that is relatively short, that presents the concepts clearly and simply, and that supports the vocabulary in context (i.e., meanings are provided as part of the text).

Multiple Texts Circle

Each member of a CALC brings information from several different texts to the discussion. This works well throughout a unit. In the beginning, multiple texts can be used to stimulate interest and engagement and to assess background knowledge. By the middle of a unit, students usually have enough basics to begin to delve into different aspects and share these with each other while maintaining a common general focus. Multiple texts also provide students with the means of participating in the discussion even when they are reading materials of different complexities and levels of sophistication. The use of multiple materials for a CALC ensures that no one is left out because of developmental reading needs.

Determining the Product or Outcome of the Discussion

To encourage genuine discussion so that real learning is taking place might be problematic for some content area subjects or for some students. Through our own working with teachers and students on content area literature discussions, we have found that four elements are necessary to encourage discussions that lend themselves to student discovery, meaning-making, and sustaining conversations in which learning takes place. These elements are important for any content area literature circle (CALC), but especially those that continue through a series of three or more literature circle meetings. These four elements (Lambert, 1995) are as follows.

The Holding Environment

A holding environment is a supportive environment in which learners feel safe to say what they are thinking and attempting to know. When scholars, theorists, or teachers discuss the idea of a community of learners, this is very much like the concept of a holding environment. With this thinking, then, comes the question of whether CALCs should have long-standing membership or if students should move from circle to circle with each new meeting. We have worked with both situations and have found that if the group memberships of all literature circles within a classroom function according to their own and the teacher's requirements, then long-standing membership is a positive element of CALCs because students build up "zones of safety" that allow them to truly engage one another and also be honest when they don't understand the content (Lipka & McCarty, 1994). We have also seen long-standing groups create requirements about participation and preparedness that surprise teachers. Frequently, students take these rules more seriously than the expectations of the teacher regarding homework and reading.

Sometimes, moving from group to group is good for the entire learning community or for individual students in particular. When groups don't solidify because of social dynamics, we have intervened so that learning can take place for all students. At other times, individual students may dominate the conversation, which lets other learners off the hook or renders them silent. We have attempted different groupings so that all students can talk, which sometimes means that all those who have a tendency to talk work with each other while the more reticent students are placed together with the teacher to help them learn how to discuss. The one grouping we do not do or encourage other teachers to do is to place students in groups according to their academic standings. We have found that with different abilities, different perspectives are highlighted in student talk.

Ultimately, CALCs rely upon a holding environment in which students feel safe to reveal themselves as learners and readers, and then holding environments can produce sustaining conversations that continually develop the learning of the community itself.

Gathering Data or Information

Gathering data or information is a natural function of CALCs. Discussion is about meaning-making, and as students come together they support one another's discoveries and knowledge acquisition. As students talk more, they become learners intent on building knowledge with and for each other, and they look for the ways the information they have brought to the circle comes together or can be connected. It cannot be emphasized enough that students need to do work prior to meeting in their literature circles. Without preparation, they have little to discuss with one another, and the meeting can quickly become unsuccessful. Chapters 4–6 explore the multiple ways that students can establish purposes for their meaning-making, and they also include ideas for how students can prepare themselves for particular types of discussions. Students can become discouraged with content knowledge learning and reading if the social aspect of sharing that information is not effective or does not benefit their overall learning of the content.

Searching for Patterns and Processes

Students also examine how they came to connect aspects of what they know with what they are now learning. Learners attempt to make bridging analogies that will allow them to add new knowledge to their existing schemata or prior knowledge. For instance, in Mr. Robine's class, the students discussed how the solar system was similar to the concentric circles students make when they throw rocks into one of the playa lakes in west Texas. The rock, like the sun, is the center of the phenomenon, but unlike the rock, which sinks from view, the sun is continually seen from each planet. The students also made the analogy of a spinning top for the earth's own circular movement. Because Mr. Robine teaches that science and math are about patterns, his students are more able to make such connections in their own discussions. Asking questions that address the large numbers connected with space—such as distance to the stars, the sun, and other planets—assures Mr. Robine that connections are being made across the curriculum.

Ability to Reflect on Learning and Thinking

Once learners have shared what they know and begin to see the different ways people understand or interpret what they read, students have the opportunity to reflect upon their own ways of thinking and learning. The eighth-grade students in Ms. Saunders' class questioned each other and themselves in their content literature circles. The questions they pondered, however, led to the group members discovering more about the topic under study. The students also reflected on their abilities to understand the material as well as how the information connected to their lives. This reflective aspect of CALCs can be difficult to attain because students are seldom asked to reflect on their learning. With support from Ms. Saunders, however, these eighth graders were able and willing to make reflection more a part of their learning.

A Genuine Discussion

The following content area literature circle (CALC) presents the elements of a holding environment in which students feel safe talking to one another honestly while searching for patterns and processes that cross their lives. CALCs in a series of three meetings can produce all four elements, but we have also noted that the groups that produce all four elements have long-standing membership and have met together throughout the year.

Discussing the problems of violence in school, a topic connected to their social studies class that was covering group dynamics, one group of boys in Ms. Saunders' class exhibited their own reflections about what they had read about student alienation. Derek, an eighth grader who remains quiet during most discussions, helped his circle come to an understanding about how student alienation may be part of young people's lives, whereas Michael came to an understanding about how he can use his knowledge as an adult. John, a recent arrival from a larger city, came to a better understanding about his place at his new school.

John: *I just think that a lot of people don't understand me because of where I come from. I mean, how many other kids are new to a school and have to, like, always prove themselves to everybody else all the time?*

Derek: *I think everyone thinks they have to prove themselves to other people, especially when you're a kid who gets in trouble. What makes any one of us in this discussion different from you?*

John: *I'm new and you aren't.*

Derek: *But all of us feel weird or alone at some time. I think we just have to remember that about ourselves and about other people. Then when we remember that, maybe we won't be so hard on each other and stuff.*

Michael: *I think it's hard to remember this, especially when most of the time we don't talk about it, in school or at home.*

John: *Yeah, and then when schools are too big, like they said in this article, it's really hard for a person to remember that there might be a lot of kids who don't feel like they belong.*

Derek: *Yeah, and we have to think about how we make things bad or good for ourselves or someone else.*

Michael: *The thing that makes me crazy about all of this is that part in the article where it says they did research on this subject in the 1970s! Why haven't they done anything? It's like the research predicted kids were gonna get violent, and then nobody did anything! Why?!*

Derek: *They might not care, or maybe there isn't any money to build all the schools the research talked about.*

Michael: *What schools? The article just said smaller schools were needed. We have a small school.*

John: *Yeah, here there's a small school 'cause that's all that's needed. We don't have many kids here. But, where I came from, they had huge schools 'cause it's cheaper to build one big school than about five little schools.*

Michael: *You know, when Ms. Saunders talked about us learning stuff to make decisions when we can vote and stuff? This is the kind of stuff we need to know.*

Listening to these three boys talk and reflect upon what they had learned in a short article about adolescent alienation brings together many of the aspects for creating genuine dialogue. Because this was a long-standing literature circle, they trusted one another to say what they felt. They also discussed the information from the article while connecting to and reflecting on their own lives. All of these processes are elements of CALCs that make real discussion possible for middle-level students.

Creating a Schedule for Content Area Literature Circles

Time is a commodity of which most teachers do not have enough. When thinking about using content area literature circles (CALCs) in your content classrooms, you may not at first see how you can add anything else to your limited time with students. Our goal is to help you see CALCs as an effective way to help you accomplish your curricular goals. Used in conjunction with other instructional strategies, CALCs facilitate students' thinking about the material they are learning in science, math, social studies, and language arts from a variety of perspectives.

Most teachers we have worked with have been able to fit an average of three CALCs in a 3-week unit of study. They plan for either 1 day a week or a series of three literature circles over 3 days toward the end of the unit that allow their students to continue a dialogue that is especially engaging or in which the concept load of the content may be especially ponderous or involved. A series of literature circles might also be planned if the content topic is one that the teacher thinks the students need as foundational knowledge for further topics or studies.

Attempting to find time for CALCs is a task most teachers must address once they have decided to make room for literature circles in their content classrooms. Because periods last anywhere from 40 to 90 minutes, we know that CALCs can be more challenging for some schedules than others. We are not suggesting, however, that teachers attempt to fit content area literature circles into their daily schedules, but that they fit them into their units of study or as part of a weekly schedule. Choosing to use CALCs for one 40-minute period a week is a possibility that many teachers can accommodate within their classrooms. In Table 2-3, we share how we would use CALCs with students who are familiar with the format. With students who are not familiar with the format, we use a scaffolding approach.

Table 2-3. Scheduling a 40-Minute Period for Content Area Literature Circles

The following time schedule works for classrooms where students are already familiar with content area literature circles.

- Teacher introduces text and establishes strategy for reading (strategies in chapters 4–8, or teacher-initiated) (5 min.)
- Students read and use self-stick notes or journal notes (Short selections—three pages—recommended for in-class reading) (12 min.)
- Students meet in content area literature circles (10 min.)
- Students share key points or questions from circles (8 min.)
- Teacher recaps learning and sets objective for next step (5 min.)

Determining Student Engagement in Content Area Literature Circles

We find that the time students spend in most content area literature circles (CALCs) depends on three factors: student engagement with the content, the materials selected, and student understanding of the purpose for the literature circle. Teachers need to consider each of these factors when planning for CALCs.

If students find the topic particularly engaging or relevant to their lives, they tend to have more to discuss and more connections to make. For instance, we observed two of Ms. Mueller's groups of sixth graders—one with four boys, the other with four girls—discussing a text they had read on the conditions of the Afghani people under the Taliban. Surprised, insulted, and passionate, these two groups discussed their reading for 40 minutes during their social studies class. This was the first time they had met as a group, but the topic was of such interest and concern for them that they spent an unexpected amount of time in their CALCs.

The difficulty of the material for a particular group of students is a factor that we have a tendency to overlook when we are excited about a topic or theme that we have selected for our students to learn. Yet if the material is more difficult, either because of the concept load or because of text structures that might be unfamiliar to students, our students will spend less time with the material and thus have less to share. If the material is easy for students to understand while also providing thought-provoking scenarios or details, students will spend more time discussing the material. At other times, however, we have watched middle-level students spend a great deal of time on difficult texts because they found the topic or the discussion interesting.

The third factor that may determine how long students spend in CALCs is the ability of the students to understand the purpose of CALCs per se. Often the first couple of literature circles will be short because students are just beginning to understand how they work. In content classrooms that have a tendency to depend on textbooks in which the questions at the end of the chapter provide the prompts for student involvement in the topic, students may rush through a literature circle because of past expectations. Then the quality of the discussion, which can depend on the group membership, is an issue that teachers will need to address with their students through demonstrations and modeling of "talk."

Table 2-4 shows one example of how Ms. Saunders used the three levels of CALCs to deepen her students' engagement in the discussion of the working conditions of children around the world. One group used the book *Stolen Dreams: Portraits of Working Children* (Parker, Engfer, & Conrow, 1998), which is a series of essays that addresses the concept of child labor, why children work, and what can be done about this type of labor. The four students in the literature circle read different parts of the book and agreed to share their understandings with the others during their first literature circle. That first meeting worked very much like the jigsaw strategy, in which students fit together the pieces of the text or information to be learned. The series of CALCs helps students to stretch their thinking and their talk in ways that not only develop concept knowledge but also helps them to learn more about their participation and learning through CALCs.

Table 2-4.   A Series of Three CALCs to Discuss *Stolen Dreams*

First Literature Circle

"Dinner Table Talk" (Atwell, 1998)
- Shared initial concepts from chapters they read to "fill in" others
- Cleared up misconceptions about child labor
- Shared general thoughts and feelings
- Created analogies to child labor
- Brainstormed issues for next meeting
- Decided to read part of the book they had not read for this first discussion (optional)

Second Literature Circle

"Going Deeper": Issues or Concept Discussion
- Discussed legal issues of child labor
- Shared ideas of prevention of child labor
- Posed questions about the necessity of child labor in developing nations

Third Literature Circle

Process Discussion: Reflections, Accomplishments, & Dynamics
- Shared journal reflections on child labor and their part in the discussion
- Listed ways they could "go deeper"
- Brainstormed how they could become more inclusive of all members' voices

Prompting Discussion
With Teacher Read-Alouds

Through teacher modeling and the use of short essays, biographies, or articles, we initiate literature circles with whole-class discussions. Students are given the same piece of work to read, then we prompt them with general questions that are appropriate for discussions about the information found in that text.

Demonstrating Discussion

Hand in hand with scaffolding students' schemata is scaffolding their understanding of how best to use content area literature circles (CALCs). Using classroom demonstrations as well as whole-class discussions, we have prepared middle-level students to work in their own small CALCs throughout the year. Teachers can also use a class read-aloud to scaffold student understanding of how to talk about content in specific ways. Selecting the materials for teacher read-alouds is one task we especially enjoy, and the other is analyzing with students the type of talk that occurred during their discussions.

Holly, working with Ms. Mueller's sixth graders in their social studies class, helped them to understand the prompt of question posing by using one common text. She selected *Building a New Land: African Americans in Colonial America* (Haskins & Benson, 2001), an informational text with short biographical and historical sketches about the hardships and the changes that transpired during the colonial period. The students were asked to use one of the three-page vignettes within the book. Holly started by reading the first paragraph aloud and then modeled the questions she had about the content. She asked the students to think about questions that could not be answered directly from the text (or at least not in that paragraph). Following her example, three students voiced other questions from the read-aloud. Checking one more time for clarification questions, Holly turned the reading over to the sixth graders, who wrote questions on pieces of paper or self-stick notes as they read. Others, using a pencil, checked the places along the reading passage that prompted queries.

The class finished reading the passage in 10 minutes and then raised their hands to pose the questions they had. Holly wrote their questions on the board, and when the board was full the students began to generate answers to some of the questions they found especially interesting. Toward the end of the period, Holly asked the students to think about what they had learned that day about discussion and about the information they had read. The next day, students were asked to follow a similar procedure with another text passage from the same book. After this independent practice, Holly asked the students to think about the types of talk that occurred in their literature circles.

This example is one way of scaffolding student understanding for CALCs. Another way is through a read-aloud in which the teacher again demonstrates while reading. Students are then asked to form small groups and use one of the question prompts from this chapter or one of the strategies that address the teacher's purpose for the CALC. Regardless of which instructional approach is used, we have found that discussing the process with the students is most beneficial. In the short discussion with the sixth graders, Holly was able to solidify what they had learned about African Americans in colonial America, but she was also able to clarify the process of question posing and why it is important for content learning. When learning processes become explicit to students, they have better control over their own learning and the challenges they may face along the way.

Selecting Materials for Read-Alouds

When considering reading aloud as a way of demonstrating content area literature discussions, the selection of the material is primary. We often "practice" discussion using current events related to the topic under study or personal choices we find interesting and wish to share with our students. We select short essays or excerpts from informational texts found in newspapers, on the Internet, or in magazines such as *National Geographic* or *Newsweek,* as well as biographies or nonfiction texts we may be currently reading. We also browse bookstores for books appropriate for our students, allowing them to borrow the book once we have hooked them with an excerpt.

Four tenets guide us when we are selecting books as read-alouds for middle-level students:

  • The selection is engaging to us as readers.
  • The selection provoked a response in us.
  • The selection is something we want to share with students.
  • The selection is at an instructional level.

If we find the topic interesting, we believe that our enthusiasm will convince our students that the selection is worth listening to and discussing. If we find the material boring, it is very hard to convince our students that it is worth the time we will spend on it.

Coupled with this interest, however, must be our response to the selection. We might find the material interesting enough to share with students, but if we cannot authentically respond to it, we have little chance of demonstrating the power of informational texts to them. Response can be in the form of disgust, anger, surprise, or incredulity. We often read something and say, "This is really hard to believe!" Thus, we bring it to our students, saying, "Listen to this—I really want to hear your ideas about this."

Wanting to hear our students' ideas is also a powerful way to involve middle-level students in the discussions taking place in math, science, geography, and social studies around the world. Bringing them to that discussion is one of the key reasons we teach and one of our motivations for using content area literature circles with middle-level learners. Harste (1994) suggests that curriculum is conversation and the differences that come from those interactions. When we find materials that provoke response in our students, conversations then push their thinking and our curricula.

Finding materials on an instructional level is also one of our considerations when choosing read-alouds. Students' instructional level is often higher than their independent reading level but lower than their frustration level. By selecting materials at the instructional level, we increase our students' listening vocabulary while also providing them with information that will push their thinking. By finding materials that address these four guidelines, we find that our students become more engaged in the content knowledge, benefit from the discussions that follow, and expand their interests in the content discipline itself.

Determining the Type of Talk in a Discussion

One final activity we do with our students before we place them in content area literature circles (CALCs) is to ask them to brainstorm the types of talk they heard during the discussion. At first this question seems confusing, but once we give them examples, middle-level learners can readily list the kinds of talk that make up CALCs. Table 2-5 lists the kinds of talk that students often generate after reading and discussing a selection from a teacher read-aloud. By asking our students to create such a list, we are showing them how much deeper their discussions are than they realize. They find this especially true when we focus on how the content can be thought about or engaged. This is often the way we begin with the particular strategies we wish to teach them about perspective, question posing, and key ideas.

Table 2-5.   Kinds of Talk Generated by Content Area Literature Circles

Connections to Self	Comparisons and Contrasts
Connections to Other Books	Questioning
Persuasion	Bridging Analogies
Examples	Generalizations
Theorizing	Hypothesizing
Listing	Problem Solving
Problem Posing	Metaphors and Similes
Summarizing	Synthesizing

Although we find that teachers need to plan around a series of curricular and social issues, we also know that our students could be included in some of our planning and implementation considerations. Scaffolding students about your expectations before they engage in CALCs will help to ease them into this type of social learning. Without discussions about group sharing, the purpose of discussion, and the issues that arise as you proceed, students may not perform at an ideal level. Addressing these elements, however, prepares students for participating in CALCs that will benefit the entire classroom community.

Issues to Address Early and Often

We have already addressed several issues that arise during content area literature circles. These involved the element of time, the limitations of a standardized curriculum, and the use of CALCs with our colleagues. Two other issues, however, need to be considered: gender issues and participation issues.

Gender Issues

At the middle level, students are going through changes that may interfere with classroom learning. One issue we have encountered deals with gender. Because many girls are beginning to think that they cannot learn math and science, we have found that "girls only" literature circles can be beneficial for girls' learning (Johnson, 2000). Sometimes we have monitored the interactions between mixed groups so that all students not only have an opportunity to share but do indeed share.

Participation Issues

Although we want all students to share in content area literature circles (CALCs), we realize that not all students talk with the same passion or the same confidence as others. Many students feel more comfortable writing or reading. Thus, this issue needs to be made explicit when students first learn about discussion and CALC participation. Striking that balance between allowing for student voice and allowing students to participate in their own ways is a matter of understanding each other as learners.

Other issues connected to participation include the nonparticipant and group construction. If students choose not to work in CALCs, we invite them to work alone. Mr. Robine had a similar problem with two students who did not participate with the rest of their group, so he asked them to work together on some of the content they were learning. Realizing that they were not "having as much fun as the others," they asked if they could rejoin their groups. Mr. Robine set up firm expectations for their participation, and in time one of the students became the unofficial group leader.

When working with CALCs in her own eighth-grade classroom, Holly discovered that she had one student who remained on the periphery of the group to which he was assigned. Asking about his participation, Holly discovered that he was too shy and did not feel confident enough to share, but he wanted to remain within a group rather than work alone. Watching from outside the circle, Miguel eventually joined it after weeks of just watching. He was, however, learning from the experience, and Holly did not want to push him away from participation by giving him an individual assignment.

Deciding what is the best way to engage young people in their learning is a balancing act that teachers need to consider each time they enter the classroom. With Miguel the best move was to allow him to participate from the sidelines. With Mr. Robine's students, the best move was to give them individual assignments. Making these decisions may be difficult, but they need to be considered according to individual learners and their comfort levels.

Another participation issue involves how groups are constructed. As we mentioned, we often allow students to choose their own groups with the disclaimer that if they are not productive, the group membership will have to change. Sometimes we place together students with various interests and academic strengths. They are then able to be more productive because they think from a variety of ways that adds to the discussion. At other times we have negotiated content literature group membership with students based on what they wish to accomplish with the information they are studying. Finally, we also discuss dealing with groups that are not productive. If a group has negative dynamics or cannot be productive, we make changes to the group rather than allow them to flounder. We make our decisions in tandem with group members so that they too can understand our reasons for changing their membership. There are times, however, when a group wishes to work out the problems they are facing, and we have acquiesced to this request when there is enough time left in our unit timeline. Ultimately, we find that paying close attention to how groups work together is a vital part of using CALCs in any classroom.

Selecting an Appropriate Assessment Tool

In chapter 8, we provide a full discussion of assessment strategies that work well with content area literature circles (CALCs). Nevertheless, it seems appropriate here to give a few general ideas as you begin or continue your thinking about using CALCs with your students.

Once learners have shared what they know with others and begin to see the diversity of how people understand or interpret what they read or view, they begin to reflect upon their own ways of thinking and learning. The eighth-grade students in Ms. Saunders' class question each other and themselves in their CALCs. The questions they ponder, however, allow students to discover more about the content under study as well as themselves as learners. They discuss their abilities to understand information and how that information connects to their lives. They also discuss attributes of the text that may have been beneficial or detrimental to their learning. This reflective nature of CALCs is often the most difficult to attain because we do not often ask our students to reflect upon their learning. By addressing this with our students, we have found that they are able and willing to make reflection a part of their learning process.

Recording CALCs is one way to ensure a detailed assessment of the work of the groups in your classroom. Having a recording allows you to listen for specific topics of discussion and to particular students. It provides you with a means of addressing specific issues with students in an individual conference setting as both of you are hearing the same discussion at the same time. For many students, hearing their talk in a CALC can be a very powerful learning opportunity, as it provides them with concrete evidence of their involvement and participation.

The following principles guide our use of tape-recording students' talk:

- Record student talk for assessment purposes.
- Don't expect the recorder to be the classroom manager.
- Record talk as part of teacher research to answer questions about student understanding, use of various learning strategies, or prompts.
- Don't make a recording if you aren't going to listen to it.
- Students will be aware of the recorder the first few times one is used, but it will lose its novelty over time.
- Students will want to hear themselves on tape, so make time for short listening periods.
- Students are fascinated by their own discussions. When discussions are transcribed, use the transcriptions for helping students to learn about their learning.

Conclusion

Using content area literature circles (CALCs) with middle-level students is an exciting endeavor. We have watched young people enthusiastically engage in their learning of science, social studies, and mathematics content in ways that continue to surprise us. Their teachers have learned to harness their students' strong need for social interaction in ways that allow the curricular mandates to be addressed while also producing a pleasurable experience for themselves and their students. Working out the details of how CALCs work best for their classrooms is still an ongoing process for the teachers we work with, but they report that it is a beneficial way for them to teach and for their students to learn. Ms. Saunders and Ms. Mueller have decided to work with CALCs more often, whereas Mr. Robine has agreed that CALCs are now a regular part of his teaching. The use of CALCs is continuing to be explored by more and more teachers with more and more positive results. Deciding to take that first step, however, is the most difficult. That step includes trusting yourself as teacher and your students as learners. Once that step is taken, however, few teachers turn back. The results are too exciting, and the challenge is too rewarding.

Chapter 3

Selecting Texts for Content Area Literature Circles

This is boring!
I don't get it!
What do all these big words mean?
What does this have to do with me?
Why do we have to read this?
I don't know half these words!
I don't care about this stuff!
I never even heard of . . . !

Too often our middle-level students greet their content area reading assignments with these kinds of questions and exclamations. Even the most dedicated middle-level students have difficulty engaging with print materials that they find cumbersome in style and/or formidable in content (Ivey, 1999). When we assign individual silent reading followed by individual silent writing of answers to textbook questions, the problems only get worse.

With so much content in our world today and the finite amount of time in any given class period for our students to discover it, understand it, take ownership of it, and learn it, our students deserve to have learning activities available to them that engage them personally and profoundly. Content area literature circles (CALCs) can do this, whether students are discussing the material in their textbooks, in a text set of multiple trade materials, or in a combination of the two.

For CALCs to work effectively, students need to have access to print materials that not only address the content under study but also connect in some way to their background knowledge and experiences as well as their reading interests and needs. Using trade materials that meet your students' diverse reading interests and needs helps them to learn how to read the different text structures found across content areas. Furthermore, these materials often provide writing models that help middle-level students learn the writing and speaking genres that are used in academic disciplines.

Mr. Robine, the science teacher we met in the last chapter, uses CALCs in his science class. He found, however, that he needed help in selecting materials that would engage his students while also providing them with multiple opportunities to read widely. For a unit on the solar system, we helped him select and collect the materials listed in Table 3-1.

Table 3-1.   Solar System, Galaxy, Universe Materials for 7th-Grade Science

TRADE BOOKS

Close Encounters (E. Scott)	*Looking at Space* (I. Graham)
1000 Facts About Space (P. Beasant)	*Stargazer* (G. Gibbons)
Cosmic Science (J. Wiese)	*The Universe* (S. Simon)
Mars (S. Simon)	*Mercury* (S. Simon)
Comets, Meteors, & Asteroids (S. Simon)	*First on the Moon* (B. Hehner)
Do Stars Have Points? (M. Berger & G. Berger)	*Stars and Planets* (J. Muirden)
Planet Earth (N. Curtis & M. Allaby)	*Venus* (S. Simon)

Planets in Our Solar System (F. M. Branley)
Race to the Moon: The Story of Apollo 11 (J. Green)
Voyager: An Adventure Through Space (J. Gustafson)
Discovering Jupiter: An Amazing Collision in Space (M. Berger)
Can You Hear a Shout in Space? (M. Berger & G. Berger)
Postcards From Pluto: A Tour of the Solar System (L. Leedy)
The Usborne Encyclopedia of Planet Earth (A. Claybourne et al.)
Mission Earth: Voyage to the Home Planet (T. Jones & J. English)
A Look at Mars (R. Spangenburg & K. Moser)
Black Holes and Other Space Phenomena (P. Steele)
Scholastic Encyclopedia of Space (J. Mitton & S. Mitton)
The Usborne Complete Book of Astronomy and Space (L. Miles & A. Smith)

WEB SITES

NASA – http://www.nasa.gov
Space Telescope Science Institute – http://www.stsci.edu
National Space Society – http://www.nss.org
The Johnson Space Center – http://jsc.nasa.gov

Once his students were given access to these materials, Mr. Robine gave them time to browse the materials and select one or two pieces to investigate further. Some students browsed in pairs through a modified partner reading situation (see sidebar) while others pursued their interests independently. Mr. Robine prompted his students to use this time to gather ideas about the solar system as well as to formulate questions they might wish to pursue.

After Mr. Robine's students had spent some time browsing and reading brief sections of the texts they had selected, he placed them in CALCs so they could discuss what they were wondering about or learning. The following is a short excerpt from a literature circle that happened fairly early in the unit. The students had been reading pieces of immediate interest to them, finding answers to questions they had generated during an earlier discussion of what they knew and wanted to learn about our universe.

Partner Reading and Browsing

In *partner reading,* two students on different reading levels read and discuss the same text together. One student will read aloud a short passage to the other, and then the two students will ask each other questions about what was just read. They also make connections to other books and other content through bridging analogies, or to their personal lives. By making these connections, students comprehend the material better, clear up misconceptions, and expand their understandings of the content and the world. *Partner browsing* works in a similar way, but when browsing, students are not reading the text from the beginning of a passage to the end, but rather becoming familiar with the book and its content, text structure, and format. Students comment to one another about their connections, questions, and concerns.

Jennifer: *The sun is 4.6 billion years old and will go on for another 4.6 billion years.*

Samuel: *Then what?*

Hector: *What if an asteroid or meteor hit the earth?*

Cherie: *I never knew we could see three galaxies without a telescope.*

Jennifer: *Oh, yeah, what are they?*

Cherie: *Milky Way, Andromeda, and Large and Small Megallanic Clouds.*

Samuel: *I've heard of the first two, but not that other one.*

Hector: *Hey, how do you say a number with 21 zeroes? The galaxy that's farthest away is 80,000,000,000,-000,000,000,000 miles away.*

Jennifer: *How many light-years is that?*

Hector: *13 billion.*

Samuel: *How do they measure light-years?*

Cherie: *Even from space the land part of Earth looks mainly green.*

Hector: *I wonder why Mars looks mainly red?*

Samuel: *Haven't they found some life on Mars?*

Jennifer: *It's amazing how many stars there are. Billions just in our galaxy.*

Cherie: *I know. Once when we went to the planetarium in elementary school, it was cool to see all the stars and how they made pictures.*

Hector: *You mean constellations? At camp once our counselor knew about those and showed us how to see them.*

Cherie: *I think it would be cool to be an astronaut.*

Although this literature circle may appear scattered at first impression, these students are not reluctant or resistant. They are engaged on several fronts, as follows:

- They are sharing the information they find in the materials they are reading.
- They are answering their initial questions and asking new ones based on the information they find.
- They are connecting the information and ideas with their own background knowledge and their own experiences.

As the unit progressed, Mr. Robine's students continued their discussions of the solar system and universe through more intense CALCs that increased their knowledge base and their enjoyment of the unit.

Defining Content Materials

Content materials are print resources, including Internet sources, that provide our students with the ideas, concepts, and facts of a content topic. Although textbooks continue to be the most prevalent type of print material used, they are beginning to be supplemented as the primary source of information by a wide variety of trade books, magazines and journals, reference books, and Web sites. The set of materials brought together for Mr. Robine's unit on the solar system and universe is a good example.

Content materials are primarily nonfiction—current, fact-based information that has been well researched and offers the most authentic and accurate knowledge that the experts in the field have at the time of publication. Although a text set might include several pieces of fiction—a few novels, short stories, poems, and picture storybooks—these must also include fact-based information or concepts that are pertinent to the unit of study. In Table 3-2, we have divided the nonfiction text structures into expository and narrative formats. These two broad categories are important to note, because most middle school students have had wide experience with narrative structures but for the most part are far less experienced with expository structures. For our purposes, *expository texts* are defined as writing that gives information through explanation, description, delineation. Narrative texts are defined as writing that recounts experiences or events in a story form with plot, characters, and setting.

Table 3-2. Nonfiction Text Structures Used in Content Studies

Expository	Narrative
single-topic trade books	autobiographies
subject-specific reference trade books	biographies
how-to trade books	diaries
reports	journals
essays	memoirs
articles	historical accounts
interviews	travel accounts
manuals	personal stories
documents	news stories
speeches	magazine stories
editorials	
brochures	
general encyclopedias	
dictionaries	
textbooks	
catalogs	

Source: Mooney (2001)

It is also important to help your students identify the language that signals various types of text structures, as indicated in Table 3-3.

Table 3-3. Words That Help to Specify the Text Structure

Sequence or Time Order	Compare and Contrast	Cause & Effect or Problem Solution
First, second, third	While	Because
Next, initially, finally	Yet, however	Since
Following that	Not only	Therefore
Previously, presently	Similarly, conversely	Eventually
Now, later	In contrast	The outcome
Before, after	More than, less than	The result
When	Most, least	Consequently
In the past	In comparison	Thus
In the future	In contrast	Hence
Eventually	Likewise, unlike	Due to
During	Also	Therefore
	On the other hand	Accordingly
		Subsequently

Criteria for Text Selection for Content Area Literature Circles

As a way to illustrate the issues involved in selecting materials for content area literature circles, we will shadow Mr. Robine as he plans for their use with his science students' study of the solar system, galaxy, and universe. When planning for this unit, Mr. Robine needed to consider five general criteria, described below.

Curricular Demands

Mr. Robine began his planning by thinking about the knowledge and understandings he wanted his students to have and the applications he wanted them to be able to make at the end of the unit. He consulted the various standards documents, including those of the National Science Foundation and his state and district, regarding this aspect of his science curriculum. Taking into consideration the students in his classes and their backgrounds and interests, he determined the following as some of the major concepts on which he wanted his students to focus:

- Compare and contrast the earth and the sun to other planets and star systems.

- Describe and explain how objects in the solar system move.
- Explain scientific theories of the origin of the solar system.

His next step was to determine what print materials he thought would best support their scientific inquiries into these major concepts. It was important that the students have more than a textbook, in order to see how different authors explain concepts and what examples and details they provide. He wanted his students to read and ultimately discuss their findings as scientists, specifically astronomers and astrophysicists.

Text Level and Structure

Rather than evaluating print materials and students in relation to levels, which have been determined by very narrow means (readability formulas and reading tests), you should think in terms of student needs. The materials in Mr. Robine's set range from those that support struggling readers to those that are written for more sophisticated readers. One of the major benefits of using a text set of multiple materials is that it offers students a choice and enables them to determine which print materials they can readily access and which are more difficult for them. It is extremely important to note here that we are not advocating leveling the books, nor are we advocating matching books with kids. Rather, we are suggesting that you provide a range of materials and guide your students in making useful choices. As Ivey (1999) suggests, it is impossible to truly level either books or students' reading development, because each individual student brings a different background to a text in terms of prior knowledge and interest. Because these factors vary so much from student to student and concept to concept, they are impossible to account for in any readability formula or measure of reading achievement. The more background and interest, the more sophisticated a text the student can access. However, it is important for the teacher to note the concept loads and vocabulary and terminology demands of each text as well as the supports the books offer for helping students to deal with the concepts and the language. By knowing the books and his students, Mr. Robine can more ably guide his students' choices. Table 3-4 illustrates the text structures represented in Mr. Robine's text set.

Table 3-4.   Text Structures Represented in Mr. Robine's Text Set

Single-topic trade books: These are expository texts. They provide concepts, supporting facts, and examples. They are written in cause-effect, comparison-contrast, ordered-sequence, or simple listing formats. The illustrations provide additional information, including relevant captions.

> *The Planets in Our Solar System*
> *Discovering Jupiter: The Amazing Collision in Space*
> *Voyager: An Adventure Through Space*
> *Close Encounter: Exploring the Universe With the Hubble Space Telescope*
> *Black Holes and Other Space Phenomena*
> *Stargazers*
> *Postcards From Pluto: A Tour of the Solar System*
> *A Look at Mars*
> *Comets, Meteors, and Asteroids*
> *Mars*
> *Mercury*
> *Venus*
> *The Universe*

Subject-specific reference trade books: These are expository texts covering a number of related issues about a central broad topic. They are written in cause-effect, comparison-contrast, ordered-sequence, or simple listing formats. The illustrations provide additional information, including relevant captions.

> *1000 Facts About Space*
> *The Usborne Complete Book of Astronomy & Space*
> *Scholastic Encyclopedia of Space*
> *Visual Factfinder: Planet Earth*
> *The Usborne Encyclopedia of Planet Earth*
> *Visual Factfinder: Stars and Planets*
> *Can You Hear a Shout in Space: Questions and Answers About Space Exploration*
> *Do Stars Have Points: Questions and Answers About Stars and Planets*

How-to trade books: These describe a process or provide directions for completing a task.

> *Cosmic Science: Gravity-Defying, Earth-Orbiting, Space-Cruising Activities for Kids*
> *Looking at Space: Facts, Stories, Activities*

Historical accounts: These are narrative texts. They relate accurately a real event in story form.

> *First on the Moon*
> *Race to the Moon: The Story of Apollo 11*

Journals: These are narrative texts that provide a personal account of a real event.

> *Mission Earth, Voyage to the Home Planet: Journals of an Astronaut and an Earth*
>   *Observer*

When selecting books based on text level and structure, we also need to determine what auxiliary materials the books contain and how well they can be used by our students. The following six factors should be considered when selecting books for middle-level students.

Graphic Content

Content materials often include graphics that support the printed text. These might include photographs, drawings, diagrams, tables, charts, and maps. This kind of text support is particularly useful to visual learners and to struggling readers. The graphics support the print in ways that often have a one-to-one correspondence. Pictures with captions, for example, can provide a wealth of information. One excellent book that Mr. Robine's students found engaging is *A Look at Mars* (Spangenburg & Moser, 2001). This single-topic trade book includes information about Mars and the exploration of Mars. It also includes photographs of Mars taken from Earth, through a telescope, and from the Viking 1 landing. It has illustrations of the Milky Way Galaxy and photographs of people and places on Earth instrumental in Mars exploration. It has tables of all of the missions to Mars, giving spacecraft, departure, and arrival dates and the supporting country. It also has a timeline of Mars explorations.

Layout and Formatting

The ratio of print to graphic content is a consideration, and there should be a range within a text set. Materials that include color are more appealing to middle-level readers. Pictures that are clearly labeled and include captions are often the most useful to students. Headings and subheadings that add clarity to the materials provide necessary support for students. Concept words printed in bold type often support students' reading as they signal to the student that they may need to slow down and spend a little extra time on the context with these concepts until they become familiar with them. It is important to have a variety in this category as well and to evaluate materials based on clarity and ease of access. *Concept load* can be a factor here as well. Concept load refers to how much information is given in particular passages. Frequently, middle-level students cannot grasp the information expected of them because too much information is given at one time and/or they do not have enough background knowledge to access it.

Inclusion of an Index

The print materials that Mr. Robine found especially useful also included an index. This provided a tool for his students, who at first found informational texts that included more than the one topic difficult to use. For example, the students who were interested in knowing more about meteors found a listing for them in the indexes of nine books in the set. Along with the word *meteor,* they found *meteorite* and *meteorologist,* which gave them extended information.

An informational book that contains an expansive index is also a valuable tool for use in content area literature circles (CALCs). When engaged in a CALC, students will typically consult printed materials to support their ideas or further their understanding about a specific topic or issue. When texts that contain an index are available, students will often choose to use those books for discussion purposes.

Inclusion of a Glossary

Other elements that Mr. Robine considered when selecting texts for his students included the difficulty of general vocabulary and concept terminology. If the material is terminology laden or uses more adult, sophisticated vocabulary, it should include a glossary to facilitate students' access to the language. In the trade books included in Mr. Robine's text set, 12 included a glossary.

Inclusion of Reference List for Further Reading

For students who want or need to go beyond the text set for information, it is key to have a starting point. Often authors will provide a list of sources they used as reference, as well as titles for further reading. Students can use these lists to find additional materials in their school library or community library. These are materials that can be included in literature circles as the students are engaged in increasingly more in-depth studies. Three of the books in the set specifically list books and/or Web sites for further investigation.

Inclusion of Information About the Author(s) and Acknowledgments

This information is particularly important for determining whether the book will contain accurate information and whether the authors possess the credentials for writing the text. This is important for both you and your students to recognize and critique. It is particularly important when your students are using Web sites as well as other materials beyond the text set. All of the materials in Mr. Robine's text set include information about the author(s) and/or acknowledgments to experts.

Students' Reading Needs

Initially, students' background knowledge and prior experiences will often determine interest. Mr. Robine's text set ranges from those materials that will pique students' curiosity even if they bring little knowledge to the text, to those that assume a fairly sophisticated background level. It is also important that some of the materials in the text set deliberately connect with middle-level students' lives in order to create interest and engagement. One of the titles in Mr. Robine's text set that does this particularly well is *Do Stars Have Points: Questions and Answers About Stars and Planets* (Berger & Berger, 1999). This trade book includes a number of questions with brief answers and supporting illustrations. For example, one of the questions is "On which planet would you roast during the day and freeze at night?" Another is "Which planet is buried under thick clouds?" These types of questions create connections with the reader's experiences with hot and cold weather and with clouds.

When considering students' reading needs, you should determine which titles in the set you will want to have multiple copies of so that students can support each others' reading of certain texts. Some of the titles you will want to use for paired reading; other titles you will want as many as five to eight copies. We find it useful to include students in the review process because they will be the ones working with the texts. For this purpose, we have created a review sheet (Appendix A) that students can fill out to become more knowledgeable about how informational texts are constructed. In Table 3-5, Bethany, one of Mr. Robine's students, reviews a book she found in the school library.

Table 3-5. **Bethany's Review of *Don't Know Much About the Solar System***

Content Literature Review Sheet

Bibliographic Information: Davis, Kenneth. (2001). Don't know much about the solar system. New York: HarperCollins.

Content and Concepts Addressed:
The planets
Definitions of the universe, galaxy, gravity
Age of earth and universe
Phases of the moon
Stars, asteroids, meteoroids, comets
Space exploration

Text Structure:
Expository, told in questions and answers

Summary (one paragraph):
This book explains in a simple way what our universe is and what is in it, such as the planets, the sun, and the stars. It also talks about the moon and the earth and gives some true and false questions to think about. Each of the planets is explained, and then the book talks about asteroids, meteoroids, and comets. The book uses simple words so anyone could understand it.

Evidence of Authenticity:
The author gave dates and Web site addresses to check information.
The author explains his interest in the solar system and there is information about what other books he has written.

Evidence of Accuracy:
The information he gives matches some of the stuff in our textbook, but he tells more details.

New Vocabulary or Terminology:
Meteoroids
Asteroids
Syzygy
Solar Eclipse

Concept Load:
Hard
Just Right—This book was just right, but
            it says it was made for kids
            6–9 years old!!

Easy

Response to the Text:
I liked this book. It explained all the terms really well and showed cartoon pictures for each term. I learned what I wanted to know about the solar system in a general way, but I would need other books to get real details about one exact thing I might study, like stars.

Text Support:
Graphics: Yes
Glossary: No—the whole book was
                    like a glossary
Index: No
Appendixes: Sort of—there are lists of
                    Web sites at the end.
References: No

Response to Visuals/Illustrations:
I liked the cartoon pictures because they explain the words pretty well, but I would like to see real pictures of all the stuff in the book. The pictures seemed to match the words and how the author said stuff.

From Bethany's example, we see that students can think about the text structure, the format of the book, the language the author uses, and how the author talks about the subject. We can also see what particular students like about informational texts and then use more books with that illustration or format style when we can.

Sometimes students steer away from longer books. For the nonfiction trade books, length does not need to be an issue because most of these materials are not necessarily meant to be read cover to cover. Rather, they have tables of contents and indexes to help the reader choose pertinent sections. This does not mean that if a student is fascinated and wants to read an entire text, he or she should be dissuaded. Again, it is a matter of students making meaningful and useful choices. The teacher's job is to facilitate students' developing the metacognitive understandings of themselves as learners and the strategies they use for reading the materials to make good choices. The bottom line is that it is important to provide a range of materials.

Cultural Representation

Another issue to consider in selecting texts for student use focuses on cultural representations. This is a significant issue for both homogeneous and heterogeneous classrooms. Within the materials for the overall study and for content area literature circles (CALCs), it is essential that many different groups are represented in the texts. Students will connect with the information and concepts much more profoundly if they see themselves included. In addition, it is important for all students, but particularly those who are in primarily homogeneous school settings, to see that the wider world includes many people who are different from them. This will facilitate the development of their understandings of the world and help them to see that there are a number of different ways that people look and live. The students will see a range of ethnicities, races, socioeconomic classes, ages, family structures, and locations. We have found that it is important to evaluate books for various biases such as race, class, gender, or disability conditions. While the focus of a text may be on the content, it is important to evaluate the examples, illustrations, and other graphics for any of these biases.

In Mr. Robine's text set, he has carefully chosen materials so that his set is inclusive and as bias free as possible. A further benefit of having his students review materials is their ability to critique them for inclusion and bias so that they bring an increased level of awareness to all of the reading that they do.

Availability of Materials

One of the most difficult aspects of teaching using trade books is the question of availability. We find that by working through a curriculum committee or with the school librarian or media resource person, we can often purchase the books for units we teach year after year. The questions that guide us in our quest for materials include the following:

- *Do I have them already in my classroom?* This question might seem ridiculous, but for those of us who often use trade books, we need to peruse our own classroom or personal libraries to make sure we don't already own the text. There are times when having duplicates is an advantage, but with limited budgets, you may wish to expand your selection rather than duplicate it.

- *Does the content area department have them?* We find that there are times when our colleagues have materials that would work well in the units we are teaching.

- *Can the materials be found in the school library?* The librarian is an excellent resource when trying to find books for content area studies. We both have worked with librarians who were more than willing to purchase materials for us, but we needed to supply titles and publishers on occasion. We found this a small price to pay for excellent texts from which our students enjoyed learning.

- *Can I find the materials in the district?* Sometimes the district may have materials or have access to materials that would work in our classrooms. At other times the district has been able to purchase the materials for us. Other schools may have what you are looking for, and by working with the district office, teachers can use materials that other schools are not using.

- *Does the public library have materials I could use?* Again, we have both worked in communities where the public libraries have been willing and able to purchase materials we could use in our classrooms. Many libraries have a request form for purchasing specific materials. All we had to do was fill out the form with the purchasing information, and our libraries added the materials we requested to their collections.

Another aspect of material availability is tied to curricular documents. Curriculum guides often come with a scope and sequence that lists the materials to be used to teach particular content or units. By discussing your request for materials with the curriculum committee either at the school or district level, you may be able to broaden the curriculum to accommodate your students' interests, needs, or learning styles. Putting together sets of multiple materials can often facilitate the purchasing of necessary curricular materials for your classroom, which in turn can be used across the school and district. Creating sets of texts for purchase can also facilitate the shift of both library and textbook expenditures to trade books and multiple materials connected to content study.

Texts That Engage Students in Grades 4–8 — A Bibliography

In Table 3-6, we list books we have found to be highly effective and enjoyable for content learning. These are materials that we have used and/or seen used in our work with the teachers and students you are meeting throughout this text as well as with others. Many of these titles can be used across content areas or for more than one unit within a specific content area. Nonfiction materials, like fiction, can become "old friends" to students when they meet them in several contexts. This is especially important for students who struggle with reading. We have listed the books in alphabetical order by title. At the end of each item we have coded them CB for chapter book, PB for picture book, or RB for reference book.

Table 3-6. Bibliography for Grades 4–8

American Heritage Book of Great American Speeches for Young People. Suzanne McIntire. Wiley, 2001. (CB)

The Bone Detectives: How Forensic Anthropologists Solve Crimes and Uncover Mysteries of the Dead. Dona M. Jackson. Little, Brown, 1996. (PB)

The Case of the Monkeys That Fell From the Trees. Susan E. Quinlan. Boyds Mills Press, 2003. (CB)

A Drop of Water. Walter Wick. Scholastic, 1997. (PB)

The Environmental Movement: From Its Roots to the Challenges of a New Century. Laurence Pringle. HarperCollins, 2000. (CB)

53½ Things That Changed the World and Some That Didn't. David West. Scholastic, 1992. (PB)

First in the Field: Baseball Hero Jackie Robinson. Derek T. Dingle. Hyperion Books for Children, 1998. (PB)

(Continued)

Table 3-6.　Bibliography for Grades 4–8 (*Continued*)

Fractals, Googols and Other Mathematical Tales. Theoni Pappas. Wide World, 1993. (CB)

The Greatest Muhammad Ali. Walter Dean Myers. Scholastic, 2001. (CB)

The History of Counting. Denise Schmandt-Besserat. Scholastic, 1999. (PB)

How Do Flies Walk Upside Down? Questions and Answers About Insects. Melvin and Gilda Berger. Scholastic, 1999. (PB)

I Never Saw Another Butterfly: Children's Drawings and Poems From Terezin Concentration Camp,1942–1944. Hana Volavkova. Schocken Books, 1993. (CB)

It's Our World, Too! Young People Who Are Making a Difference: How They Do It—How You Can, Too. Phillip Hoose. Farrar, Straus and Giroux, 1993. (CB)

Lakota Woman. Mary Crow Dog. HarperCollins, 1990. (CB)

Lou Gehrig: The Luckiest Man. David A. Adler. Harcourt, 1997. (PB)

The New Way Things Work: From Levers to Lasers, Windmills to Web Sites: A Visual Guide to the World of Machines. David Macaulay. Houghton Mifflin, 1998. (RB)

The Number Devil: A Mathematical Adventure. Hans Magnus Enzensberger. Holt, 1997. (CB)

One Grain of Rice: A Mathematical Folktale. Demi. Scholastic, 1997. (PB)

Peace and War: A Collection of Poems. Michael Harrison and Christopher Stuart-Clark. Oxford

University Press, 1989. (CB)

Sir Cumference and the Sword in the Cone: A Math Adventure. Cindy Neuschwander. Charlesbridge, 2003. (Series) (PB)

Space Station Science: Life in Free Fall. Marianne J. Dyson Scholastic, 1999. (CB)

Stories From Where We Live [Series]: The California Coast, The Great Lakes, The Great North American Prairie, The Gulf Coast, The North Atlantic Coast. Sara St. Antoine. Milkweek, 2003. (CB)

There Comes a Time: The Struggle for Civil Rights. Milton Meltzer. Scholastic, 2001. (CB)

The Usborne Encyclopedia of Planet Earth. Anna Claybourne, Gillian Doherty, and Rebecca Treays. Scholastic, 1999. (RB)

Voices From the Fields: Children of Migrant Farmworkers Tell Their Stories. S. Beth Atkin. Scholastic, 1993. (CB)

Wild Technology: Inventions Inspired by Nature. Phil Gates. Kingfisher, 1995. (CB)

Words That Built a Nation: A Young Person's Collection of Historic American Documents. Marilyn Miller. Scholastic, 1999. (CB)

Conclusion

Wide reading and many opportunities to discuss what is read in their content area literature circles (CALCs) will facilitate students' continuous literacy development as well as deeper content knowledge and learning. Thus, you need to have materials that are readily accessible as well as developmentally challenging to each and every student. We want to strongly suggest that leveling and labeling do not accomplish meeting the diverse needs of your students as readers. Rather, this is accomplished by providing choices and by guiding those choices. Struggling readers often lack confidence as much if not more than they lack skill. They need many opportunities to read at a level of comfort and to add information and ideas to the literature circles in which they participate. Being able to participate fully in their classes will go a long way toward speeding up their literacy growth. Those students who are too often bored and for whom everything seems to come too easily can be readily challenged at an appropriate level. With guidance and an occasional push, every middle-level student should be reading and working at a level that promotes continuous literacy, and cognitive, intellectual, social, and emotional growth and development. CALCs, in which students are discussing what they know and what they have trouble understanding, pushes the students to think and to grow as content learners.

It is encouraging and exciting to think about how informational texts and text sets that include a variety of materials can open the door to content learning for all students. With the vast array of content materials readily accessible to teachers, schools, and school districts, the learning of content topics has never been so engaging or so exciting.

Chapter 4

Highlighting Key Ideas in Content Area Literature Circles

Content subjects are similar to cultures. The patterns of thought, behavior, and ways of being in mathematics may be similar to those of science or social studies, but they still have a separate identity that is based on what that content area finds important and what principles guide its processes. Middle-level students need to become aware of how the information of a specific content area subject works, what experts in its field investigate, and how those experts go about thinking about the world and their subject. Discussing such matters in content area literature circles (CALCs) guides students toward understanding more deeply the information they are expected to learn. Through CALCs, students learn to think and talk like those experts who have made mathematics, science, and social studies their lives.

In this chapter, we will explore strategies for helping middle-level students to access and discuss key ideas in their CALCs.

Thinking Like a Historian

Historians ask some of the following questions when they read:

- What other perspectives are there on this event?
- What may have caused this event?
- What are the outcomes of this event?
- Who was involved?
- How does this connect to other events during that period?
- What else was happening during this period?
- Could such an event happen at this time?
- How does this event change my thinking about current social, political, and economic conditions?
- What can the present age learn about our culture, society, or government from this event?

Helping Students to Discuss Key Ideas in Content Area Literature Circles

One way to deepen middle-level students' thinking about content is to have them first focus on finding the key issues, big ideas, and major attributes included in the print material. Once they have done that, talking about these elements in content area literature circles will help them to sort out their misconceptions about the reading while also highlighting the ideas they found of interest.

The Definition of Key Ideas

When thinking about key ideas, we find that many teachers consider them to be the main ideas determined by the author or the text. There are, however, additional aspects of reading that could also fall under the umbrella term *key ideas*. These include the big ideas that a reader may generalize from the material; these issues may or may not be stated in the text, but they can be found when reading between the lines or critically questioning a text. They also include the major attributes of the text, including the formatting, figures, and graphs, as well as the photographs that have been included in the text to support the prose. How content is presented can be a question that middle-level teachers and students may wish to consider when reading from a critical perspective. Table 4-1 gives examples of key issues and ideas as well as major attributes of the reading that students might consider when reading.

Table 4-1.   Defining Key Issues, Big Ideas, and Major Attributes

Key issues are the main concepts presented in the print material.

Example: The current state of orangutans is precarious.
                  Impact of the orangutans' shrinking environment
                  Relations of orangutans and humans

Big ideas consist of textual information that supports the key issue.

Example: Orangutans are shy animals and not very social.
                  Human societies are encroaching on the orangutans' habitat.
                  Orangutans remain solitary for most of their adult lives.

Major attributes are the structural elements that the author uses to share the key issues and big ideas.
Example: The nonfiction narrative structure (in which Birute Galdikas, the real-life character, acts within the setting of the orangutans' habitat) clearly delineates and illustrates the key issues and big ideas.

The Importance of Determining Key Ideas

Sharing their finding of these elements provides students with the opportunity to connect with their prior knowledge, build interest, and share their understandings, curiosity, and growing enthusiasm for the content. Once they have established the key issues, big ideas, and major attributes, they have a framework in which to place additional information that helps them to understand the material in a more comprehensive way.

By having students talk about the issues and ideas, you can more naturally lead them into discussions about the major attributes of the text and how these can help them to determine the purpose for their reading as well as how to approach the information for better comprehension.

Through a discussion of the attributes or text structures of a particular text, students come to understand the ways in which content is presented. They focus on photographs, graphs, and figures as well as some of the more basic components of many information texts, such as the table of contents, glossary, and index. These attributes, which also include different font styles (such as boldface) and sizes, direct readers toward knowledge they might not have noticed when reading through the written text. We have found that many middle-level students have more difficulty with texts that contain these elements because they do not know how to make use of these attributes, or because they have not been asked or taught to make use of these essential parts of many textbooks or informational trade books as well as other nonfiction materials. Once students understand the meanings of key issues, big ideas, and major attributes of the print material, they are not only more prepared to discuss the text in a global and metacognitive manner but are also better able to put the pieces of a text together.

Developing Metacognition

A particular process that students need to notice the text, and thereby become more skilled as readers, is metacognition. *Metacognition* is literally "thinking about thinking," and it involves both positive and negative aspects of our reading, some of which are the following:

- Realizing what information we know as we read
- Noting when we become bogged down
- Finding out where and when we lost interest in the material
- Recognizing connections we make with other readings and our experiences
- Noticing when we are just looking at words and not comprehending
- Identifying when we need more prior knowledge to understand the information
- Recognizing how we connect with the information we are reading
- Discovering that previously unknown words become familiar through exposure
- Noting when our mind begins to wander

An Example of Determining Importance From Mathematics

To begin a study on exponential growth, Mr. Elliott read aloud the folktale *One Grain of Rice* (Demi, 1997) about a young girl in India who outsmarts a selfish raja by asking for one grain of rice, to be doubled each day for a month. Elliott's sixth-grade students wrote quickly in their math journals about their impressions and initial thinking about the content of the book. The following excerpt presents Renee's thoughts about the read-aloud and how it related to mathematics. She also addresses her thinking while listening to the read-aloud, which brings in her metacognitive awareness during the reading event.

> As Mr. Elliott was reading, I made a connection to what my dad did to me with pennies and my allowance. He said he would double the amount every week, but I had to start with a penny, and I said no way. The amount gets so much bigger so much quicker. I had never really thought about it this way before. Then, as Mr. Elliott was reading more, I was asking questions about how exponents work. I'm still not quite sure how those little numbers, those exponents, work. I guess they make numbers and things get bigger quicker like in the story. The story was making me think of science and the way cells grow when they split apart and then the new ones split apart and so on.

Through their journaling, Mr. Elliott's students became better prepared for discussing the content he wants them to learn when they meet in their content area literature circles (CALCs). The following list shows the benefits that Mr. Elliott's students reap from journaling about the content before attending their CALCs:

Focuses thinking

Summarizes content

Formulates questions

Highlights key terminology

Synthesizes ideas

Identifies misunderstandings

Creates intertextual connections to life and other content

Reflects on literacy and content strategies

After the students finished their quick writing, Mr. Elliott asks them to get into their long-standing literature circles and share their impressions, connections, and ideas. In the course of this discussion time, the members of one particular group showed their growing understandings of exponential growth by connecting with their life experiences:

Renee: *This is like the trick my dad played on me to get me to do yard work. I didn't get it then. He told me he'd pay me by giving me a penny the first time we worked and then double it every time after that.*

Sarah: *I would have said, "No way!"*

Renee: *That's what I said, too. And he said, you'll be sorry. And I was after he explained how it would work. Now I see it even better.*

Sarah: *Yeah, you'd be rich and he'd be broke.*

Elena: *I think I'll see if my parents will go for this offer. They're always yelling at me to clean my room.*

After this initiating literature circle, Mr. Elliott put the term *exponential growth* on the class word wall and asked each group to briefly share their ideas about the content of the read-aloud. Using the examples that the students shared, he then moved into the mathematical concepts involved in the concept of exponential growth. Because of their participation in a CALC, the students could now think and discuss in a more focused manner the concepts they were learning about in their math class.

Strategies for Helping Students to Address Key Ideas in Content Area Literature Circles

By finding the issues, ideas, or attributes that are directly addressed in the readings or inferred by students as they read, the students can gain a greater understanding of the content concepts found in the narrative and expository texts used in their content classes. Three initiating strategies that enable students to do this include "say something," think-alouds, and graphic organizers. Through demonstrations as well as invitations or activities that involve individual students or the entire class, you can help your students to understand how knowledge acquisition and comprehension require metacognitive awareness. By learning to use these strategies, students will become more aware of what they are doing as they read, and they will then be more able to highlight the key ideas in their reading. Students will also realize how good readers unconsciously work these strategies into their reading process.

"Say Something"

One of the first strategies we use to teach our students about key ideas, and how to attend to them, is the strategy "say something" (Short et al., 1996). By saying something to a partner when they read, or by writing something on self-stick notes for discussion later, students become more aware of the key ideas in a text as well as their thought processes during reading. They then learn to concentrate on the ideas in the text. We have found that because of what students bring to the reading, they may have different ideas of what is a key idea. We allow students to discuss these ideas in content area literature circles (CALCs) and then ask our students to list the three ideas they believe are the most important. Each CALC group shares with the rest of the class, and we fill in any gaps they may have missed in their discussions. Because students justify their ideas in CALCs and then the group justifies why their three ideas are the key ideas in a text, they are working more closely and deeply with the content. By discussing our ideas as a whole class, students learn what the key ideas are as well as address how the differences they bring to the text can develop a variety of answers. The following description (Short et al., 1996) explains how "Say Something" is used in CALCs (see chapter 6 for an example of this strategy):

> In pairs or trios, students read the same short piece of text together. They "chunk" the material into sections (one to three paragraphs per chunk) and determine whether to read each chunk silently or take turns reading the chunks aloud. Following the reading of each chunk, they stop and say something to each other in connection with the issues, ideas, and attributes in that chunk. The "something" can take the form of a question, a comment about text structure, a connection with personal experiences or to other texts or chunks of the text being read, an alternate perspective, or a prediction of what's next. They can also write down each other's comments in note form so that they have a record of their "say something."

The following excerpt is from a conversation students had after reading about stereotypes. Ms. Saunders, their teacher, asked them to think about their own stereotypes and to "say something" in response to what they had read.

J.D.:   *My cousin is an epileptic and I don't think she is as smart as all the rest of us.*

Sam: *I don't think it has anything to do with intelligence.*

Julius: *What makes people intelligent, anyway? Genes, or is it something else, like getting a good education?*

J.D.:   *But that's my point. What if there is something that keeps you from learning?*

Sam: *I think I'm pretty smart in science, but I don't do so good in English. I don't like the books we have to read. So am I smart or what?*

Julius: *Maybe we are all smart in some ways and not so smart in other ways.*

Sam: *And probably epilepsy doesn't have anything to do with any of it!*

Julius: *This book on the brain [Brain by Seymour Simon] does say some pretty cool stuff about how the brain works.*

Sam: *I am thinking the brain is pretty complex because Albert Einstein was like, the smartest person in the world, and he had a tough time with school.*

J.D.:   *How do you know that about Albert Einstein? Are you sure? I just need to get more information on epilepsy before I start saying if someone is smart or not.*

Sam: *I looked up Albert Einstein. And he was smart enough, but he was bored all the time. So he just used to skip school.*

J.D.:   *I got on the Internet and looked up epilepsy and famous people and there was a cool site called epilepsiemuseum. I found out that a lot of smart people had epilepsy.*

Julius: *Like who?*

J.D.:   *Like your boy Caesar. So did, uh, like Charles Dickens, Socrates, and even Danny Glover. You know, the guy from Lethal Weapon.*

Sam: *Let's ask Ms. Saunders if we can get on the computer right now and look up that Web site.*

J.D.:   *And some of the other ones, too.*

From their initial sharing through "say something," these students began to internalize some of the key ideas that Ms. Saunders wanted them to learn about stereotyping in their own lives. As an added benefit, these students also became more curious about epilepsy, Albert Einstein, and other famous people who defied J.D.'s initial thoughts about those who have epilepsy.

Think-Alouds

Thinking aloud helps me see how I should
be working with the words when I read.

—Sally, fifth-grade student

The think-aloud strategy is a powerful tool for building students' development of metacognitive awareness and increasing the learning potential of their content area literature circles (CALCs). Thinking aloud is exactly what it sounds like—learners share orally the thoughts, ideas, questions, or connections they make as they read or work through problems or issues in their heads. By demonstrating this for students, we show how proficient readers and thinkers are always thinking, predicting, wondering, or wrestling with elements within a reading. The primary objective of thinking aloud is to make explicit the processes readers go through as they work out the text before them.

Jeffrey Wilhelm (2001) notes as follows:

> The most powerful thing we can teach is strategic knowledge, a knowledge of the procedures people use to learn, to think, to read, and to write. The most effective way to introduce students to how to use these tools is to model them in the contexts of meaningful tasks and then to assist students in their own use of these strategies (p. 7)

The following are prompts that you can use with your students to set the think-aloud process in motion:

- I think this means . . .
- This connects with . . .
- I have a picture in my mind of . . .
- This reminds me of . . .
- My question about this is . . .
- I think the next idea or example will be about . . .
- I disagree with the author about . . .
- I'd like to know more about . . .

In the following pages, we present three examples of how think-alouds work. One of the examples, Jane Addams and Hull House, concerns a social studies content text; the other two show how to use a think-aloud in a mathematics and a science classroom.

As students read or listen to the teacher read aloud, we suggest that they use self-stick notes to remember their thoughts, questions, and connections for our post–think-aloud discussion. The use of these notes can help students to keep track of the thinking they are doing at particular points in the text by having them think aloud on paper or write in their journals. We call it "thinking aloud" because they pause and write something on their self-stick notes to share with others later. This use of thinking aloud requires that they stop and jot down the thought as it occurs and note exactly where in the text they stopped by placing the note in close proximity to that part of the text. We use this strategy frequently and ask our students to use self-stick notes mostly when they are first learning about metacognition. As they become more proficient with the way the reading process works, we invite them to use fewer self-stick notes and use them as discussion starters about the content of the text.

Example: Thinking Aloud in Social Studies

In this example we will look at how we use some of the prompts to make our thinking visible as we are reading. The following vignette is an example of how we worked with a short passage from *Words That Built a Nation* (Miller, 1999). The passage, entitled "Twenty Years at Hull House" (p. 88), considers the work of Jane Addams, a reformer who created settlement houses for the poor in the late 1800s and early 1900s. Since we knew very little about Jane Addams, we thought that this passage would be useful in showing how we would think aloud through content of which we had little knowledge. The information from the book is in boldface, whereas our response—our thinking aloud—is in italics. We followed up our think-aloud demonstration with a brief description of the characteristics of that particular response to show how readers address issues of vocabulary, unknown concepts, and personal connections as they read.

By the late 1890s increasing numbers of American reformers were focusing on helping the urban poor.

I have a couple of questions about this sentence. First, what exactly is a reformer? I noticed that they focused on helping the urban poor in the 1890s; what did they do before that? Did they ever help the rural poor? I also have a comment. I am glad to see that Americans have been concerned about others throughout out history.

This comment addresses the vocabulary used. Often, students don't know and don't question what particular words mean in a specific context. By thinking aloud about vocabulary, teachers show students that we all have questions about how words are being used.

The reformers organized community centers in slum areas, where many immigrants lived.

There are many concepts in this sentence of which I am unsure of the meaning. What does community center mean here? When I think of community center, I think of the YMCA, or small centers in many neighborhoods where people take classes like aerobics or watercolor painting. Wow! That's amazing if Jane Addams was the person who started this idea. I also wonder about slum areas. I have heard of ghettos, projects, and urban neighborhoods but don't know if they all mean the same thing. I wonder if today's immigrants live in similar circumstances. The sentence also says "reformers." I wonder how many there were and how they all got together. I wonder why the author doesn't say more about these people, like some of their names.

This response shows how the reader connected the passage to her current world in the hope of figuring out some of the concepts unfamiliar to her. By sharing these kinds of connections with students, teaches give students permission to make the materials they are reading relevant to their lives. By doing so, students have an easier time remembering the information they have read.

The centers, or settlement houses, offered neighborhood people services and guidance. In 1889 Jane Addams and her college friend Ellen Starr founded Hull House on Halstead Street, in one of Chicago's worst slums.

I wonder why they were called settlement houses in the beginning. I wonder what those houses were like. I am also thinking about how Jane Addams and Ellen Starr were friends in college. I wonder if they were thinking about the poor and the immigrants while they were still at college. That's pretty amazing because they would have been really young when they came up with their ideas. I wonder how they got the funding for the settlement houses.

These thoughts give students insight into how the reader connects to other concepts as well as the historical context of the piece. Students have a difficult time with contextualizing the information they read. By asking questions of ourselves as readers about setting and historical context, we expand our interest and our knowledge of the material.

Addams and the other settlement workers lived in Hull House. It grew to have a nursery, a kindergarten, a gymnasium, and a playground, and offered activities such as music and art

classes. By 1900 about 100 settlement houses had been established across the country. Hull House served as a model for many of them.

Why did they call it Hull House? And from the description, it sounds a lot like today's community centers across the country. I wondered about that a couple of sentences ago. It says Hull House was a model for those 100 other houses. I wonder if they all did the same things, or if particular services were offered because of the specific needs of the neighborhood. I want to know where those other houses were.

This response shows how the reader is connecting the information from one part of the passage to the next. Good readers are constantly summarizing the material as they read.

Addams's work caused many Americans to support the need for social reform. Today, largely because of her efforts, community centers and settlement houses exist in cities across the United States.

I wonder how they advertised Addams's work? This sentence says many Americans supported the need for social reform. I wonder what social reform means. That's something I will have to do more reading on. And I was right! Addams did start the idea of community centers like the one in my neighborhood. That's so neat! Now I feel like I know how part of my neighborhood began.

Here the reader confirms a question she had asked earlier as she was reading. Again, good readers constantly predict and confirm or disconfirm the information they are reading.

This example shows how we, as good readers, are always thinking, wondering, questioning, and connecting to the written text—if we comprehend the information as we read. If we do not, then the words may not actually register in our consciousness. We might be pronouncing the words, or our eyes might be going over the words, but we are not thinking about our reading; our minds are elsewhere. To be aware of our thinking, wondering, predicting, and connecting, we need to know when we understand the text and when we are just looking at words—in other words, being metacognitively aware. An understanding of these metacognitive strategies is significant in terms of CALCs as the students share much of this thinking as they work through their knowledge acquisition, understanding, and application of the material under discussion and the concepts under study.

Through teacher and classroom demonstrations of thinking while reading, students can build the habit of being conscious of what they are doing while reading. They will also concentrate on the key ideas in the text and be more apt to remember those ideas. We use a Thinking During Reading form (Appendix B) to help students acquire the habit of attending to their thinking while reading while also giving them a place to gather and record their thoughts. They take these sheets to their CALCs to discuss with others who have also read the same material. The ensuing discussion allows all members to adjust their misconceptions or deepen their knowledge of the main ideas found within a selection. Table 4-2 is an example of one eighth grader's Thinking During Reading form, part II.

Table 4-2.   Thinking During Reading Form, Part II

Name: Melissa   Date: March 13
Title of Book: *Girls Think of Everything: Stories of Ingenious Inventions by Women*
Reason for Reading This Book: I was doing a science report on inventions and I wanted to read about what girls or women did to invent some things.

Three Ideas to Share in CALC:

1. Ruth Wakefield invented chocolate chip cookies and when she did, the Nestle® company decided to invent chocolate chips just for her cookies because she was just breaking up candy bars.

2. One of the youngest girls to invent something was Becky Schroeder. She invented Glo-Sheets® that let you write in the dark.

3. A lot of inventions were discovered because the inventors said they were a mistake. One example is Liquid Paper® and another example is chocolate chip cookies.

After CALC

New Ideas From Others:

1. Other inventions are made by accidents that happen in the labs or at home.

2. Women have contributed to a lot of things, not just inventions. Women marched for the vote and they had political ideas to help people. Their inventions helped people, too.

3. Lilly shared a book about women and what they did during the 1890s to 1920s. I need to look at that book. It's called New Paths to Power.

How Discussion Helped Me Understand:

By talking to Lilly and Sarah, I found out that women did a lot of things that are important to us. They told me about how women worked during World War II and about how women made changes in our country and in the government.

(Continued)

Table 4-2.   Thinking During Reading Form, Part II (*Continued*)

Further Use
How This Information Will Help With My Project:
I think what I can do is start my paper on inventions with an introduction about how women have worked and been an important part of all parts of the world, like in history, government, and science. Then I will use one of Lilly's examples and one of Sarah's.

It may take many teacher demonstrations of thinking aloud, as well as many classroom opportunities for students to record their thoughts as they read. We do not recommend, however, that the Thinking During Reading form become a regular part of your classroom structure. We used it when first asking students to share the key ideas in their readings during their CALCs and when first discussing think-alouds. Some students found that it helped them with inquiry projects, and so they would continue to use the form even after we no longer required it. Discussions of their readings, learning logs about what they have read, and semantic maps of connections they made while reading are also good ways to make students aware of how one must think while reading.

Example: Thinking Aloud in Math

> *Comprehension is very important. One of the important things, especially for mathematics, is to think aloud to model your comprehension strategies so that students can understand how you work through a problem, and then they may be able to start doing it themselves.*
>
> —Mr. Elliott, sixth-grade math teacher

Think-alouds are a natural fit for science and social studies but may not seem so for math, at first glance. However, teacher demonstrations of thinking aloud will also work in this situation. With math concepts, students need to know when they are not connecting, what they do not understand in the mathematics formula, or what particular words don't make sense to them. We have found that by thinking aloud math formulas in explicit patterns, students have a better idea of how the process or formula works. Yet there are times when knowing the formula may not be enough.

Sometimes we can see a variety of ways to think through a problem. What, then, makes the most sense for solving that problem?

Sometimes the think-aloud becomes the focus of the CALC. By thinking aloud, students can show each other how they processed the problem, which expands the way others in the group can think about how to solve problems in the future. The following vignette shows how a group of sixth-grade students worked through a problem on data collection and statistical analysis. The students are reading across texts that provide examples of data collection to solve a particular problem. The students are asked to bring both their sources and the information to the literature circles. Mr. Elliott, the math teacher, has asked his students to answer the question, "Is anyone typical?"

> What are the characteristics of a typical middle school student? Does a typical middle school student exist? What kinds of data might you collect to help you answer these questions? How might you collect this data? Once you have collected the data, how might you analyze it and interpret it?

Mr. Elliott told us that he wanted his students to work on a number of mathematical concepts with this problem. These concepts included the following:

- Creating a coordinate graph to plot two variables
- Organizing data in different ways (table, line plot, stem and leaf plot, bar graph)
- Understanding mean, median, mode, and range and their differences in relation to the concept of "average"
- Labeling data as numerical or categorical

As the students made decisions about what to research, Mr. Elliott made available a set of materials for students to consult that would help them with their thinking and the mathematical tools they would be using to gather data, analyze it, and report their findings. He also made the computer terminals available to students or groups that wanted to use the Internet for finding information. The materials he included in his text set are listed in Table 4-3.

The project was twofold. The students needed to understand the research and math tools they were going to use, and they needed to develop surveys to collect the necessary information to answer their inquiry questions. As they read from the materials Mr. Elliott had for them, they also filled out sections of the Thinking During Reading form that were relevant to the task they were doing. This research about the typical middle school student continued for the rest of the period. Mr. Elliott then asked the students to be ready to share from their Thinking During Reading forms in CALCs the next day.

Table 4-3.   Mathematics Texts for Content Area Literature Circles

Mathematics Illustrated Dictionary: Facts, Figures and People Including the New Math (J. Bendick, M. Levin, and L. Simon, 1972)

The I Hate Mathematics! Book (M. Burns, 1975)

Discovering Graph Secrets: Experiments, Puzzles, and Games Exploring Graphs (S. Markle, 1997)

Reading the Sports Page: A Guide to Understanding Sports Statistics (J. R. Feinberg, 1992)

Math Wizardry for Kids: Solve Puzzles, Play Games, Have Fun! Surprise Yourself With Your Own Wizardry (M. Kenda and P. S. Williams, 1995)

Math Smart Junior: Math You'll Understand (M. Lerner and D. McMullen, 2002)

Graphs (D. Lowenstein, 1976)

How Math Works: 100 Ways Parents and Kids Can Share the Wonders of Mathematics (C. Vorderman, 1976)

As the students formed their CALCs, it was evident that they were eager to share what they had learned and what they were thinking in relation to facilitating their group's answering the question they had posed. The group investigating pet ownership brought both their Thinking During Reading forms and the books they were reading.

Naomi: *I think we ought to construct our survey so that we can easily chart our data.*

Bryan: *Ok, but I want to be able to make a graph that shows percentages.*

Matt: *Are we going to distinguish between family pets and the ones that actually belong to the specific kid?*

Bryan: *Here's an example of a graph we could use.*

Angela: *Ok, but shouldn't we have our survey first? What are our questions?*

Bryan: *Well, one thing is do they have a pet or not.*

Naomi: *Yeah, and then we could ask if they do, what kind.*

Bryan: *Okay, let's write them down.*

At the end of this lesson, Mr. Elliott asked the students to write in their learning logs what they had learned though their thinking sheets and their CALC so they would remember the major concepts connected to data collection and statistics in the future.

Seeing how well the Thinking During Reading form worked, and how demonstrating thinking aloud about gathering and reporting data helped the students with their math concepts, Mr. Elliot decided to make thinking aloud a greater part of his teaching. He found that by demonstrating his thinking, students become aware of how capable mathematicians, scientists, readers, and writers process the knowledge intimately involved in their content areas or fields of study. He also realized that students do help each other when sharing their own thinking through think-alouds in literature circles. As students share their ideas, they notice the attributes of mathematical texts as well as the key issues and big ideas involved when attempting to solve problems.

Example: Thinking Aloud in Science

> When we talk with each other about the stuff we are learning, we get more out of it. We learn more and we figure out what we didn't learn, too. That helps me to understand what I usually concentrate on in a book and what I'm missing. For instance, one of my group partners always looks at the pictures and the figures in the books we read, and I never do. She tells me the stuff she is learning and how she found out that stuff, and I think, "Man, I have to look at the pictures and other stuff in the books. Not just the words." I have to concentrate on remembering that, so I can do better in class, and in our content circles.
>
> —Lester, age 13

In Mr. Graham's sixth-grade science class, the students are beginning a study of ecosystems. The set of materials includes a diversity of topics, which allows the students to study the ecosystems themselves as well as particular aspects of each ecosystem. These texts are presented in Table 4-4.

Table 4-4. Texts Used in Ecosystem Unit

Tree of Life: The World of the African Baobab (Bash, 1989)
Antarctica (Cowcher, 1990)
Caves (Wood, 1990)
Cactus Hotel (Guiberson, 1991)
The Ever-Living Tree: The Life and Times of a Coast Redwood (Vieira, 1994)
The Kingfisher Young People's Book of Oceans (Lambert, 1997)
Flashy Fantastic Rainforest Frogs (Patent, 1997)
Fur, Feathers, and Flippers: How Animals Live Where They Do (Lauber, 1994)
When the Tide Is Low (Cole, 1985)
Into the Sea (Guiberson, 1996)
Letters From the Canyon: An Alphabetical Visit to the Grand Canyon (McAnally, 1995)

A range of materials also allows all students to add to the CALC conversations no matter what their reading needs. In this classroom, the students browsed and jotted down things they were familiar with and made connections to things they had experienced. Mr. Graham allowed the students 15 minutes of browsing and connecting. He then invited them to gather in CALCs according to the ecosystem of the books they browsed.

Although Mr. Graham usually organized the students into CALCs according to the topics they had been reading about—such as (a) larger ecosystems like oceans or forests, (b) particular continents like Antarctica, and (c) particular animals in specific ecosystems— he also placed his students in what he termed "initial CALCs" right after browsing so they could share their first thoughts about what they were learning. In the following literature circle, four students begin to connect the information from their readings while also discussing their questions from their thinking aloud during browsing:

Margaret: *What information did you find of interest?*

Lester: *I was reading this book called* Wolves, *and in it the author says that wolves adapt to different climates and different surroundings. I'm thinking they could be parts of any kind of ecosystem. I kept thinking, "Could wolves really live, like, where we are?"*

Shirley: *Yeah, they could live here, but they would probably be shot. And wolves don't really live in all ecosystems, like the ocean.*

Rosa: *I was reading with Lester, and we found out that wolves hang out in, um, social groups like people, so they're like families, but every once in a while one hangs out by himself. That's called a lone wolf. I wondered why that happens and if it is dangerous. Then I got to thinking about people who don't hang out with other people, but that's really kind of rare. Then I was thinking how some people are called lone wolves, too.*

Margaret: *Maybe because the lone wolf doesn't fit in with the group, like he might be too strong or too weak for the group to like him.*

Shirley: *Hey! Are all lone wolves the boys?*

Rosa: *I don't know, but I think they might be because the females always run off with another male and start a new group.*

Lester: *So, wait a minute, when it comes to ecosystems, some animals are only particular to certain ecosystems, but the wolf, isn't, right?*

Margaret: *There are all different kinds of wolves, so they can live in the desert, or the mountains, or the tundra, all kinds of places.*

Shirley: *Wolves can be important to many different kinds of ecosystems. That's pretty cool when you think about it. Sometimes they can help an ecosystem even when humans don't think they do.*

Rosa: *What do you mean?*

Shirley: *It's like in some of the more western states, like Montana and Wyoming, the wolves actually help the elk population stay down—*

Lester: *And even the mouse or rodent population when they can't get elk. I saw that in a movie one time.*

Shirley: *Okay, but like I was saying, they keep the elk population down, but some of the ranchers think they are dangerous to their cattle. Are the wolves dangerous to the cattle, really?*

Margaret: *It would be hard to convince a rancher that when a wolf pack killed one of his cows, the pack was just keeping the population of cows down!*

Lester: *Ha! They sure wouldn't think that was funny. But they do kill the old and sick, mostly in the elk herds.*

Rosa: *At Yellowstone, they reintroduced the wolf and now I'll bet the ecosystem is changing.*

Margaret: *Good thought! Ecosystems do change, just like families when kids come and go, or when someone dies.*

Lester: *I would never have compared an ecosystem to a family. What a weird way to think of it, but it kind of works, I guess.*

Listening to these students talk, we found that they had burgeoning ideas about ecosystems, and they easily discussed their questions and answers with each other. The students were able to further discuss what issues, ideas, and attributes they found in the texts they read that addressed ecosystems. The positive aspect of this conversation was that students were expanding one another's knowledge base of wolves and how they fit into an ecosystem through the questions and answers they discussed. With further discussion, they were able to sort out which ecosystem they wanted to study.

Graphic Organizers

> *It was pretty cool sharing our different organizers with each other. I mean, I like words, so I did a Frayer model on the tundra, but Shirley likes pictures, so she did more diagrams, such as the pyramid. Then Margaret, she likes words, too, but she likes to think about bigger ideas and then smaller ideas in a different way than I do, so she did a semantic map. It is pretty amazing how people think differently about what we learn. But I like how we can all learn from each other—not just about wolves or ecosystems or whatever, but how to think about what we are reading.*
>
> —Rosa, age 14

Another strategy for facilitating students' comprehension of the key issues, big ideas, and major attributes in their content reading requires students to put this initial information into a graphic organizer. As the students read, they think about how the information should best be organized. There are a number of graphic organizer formats that students should be familiar with and have available for use (Table 4-5). They should also have the freedom to make up their own.

Table 4-5.   Types of Graphic Organizers

Analogy Graphic Organizer

Compares two concepts by listing their similarities, differences, and categories.

Concept Mapping

Helps with concept definition by asking: What is it? What is it like? What are some examples?

Different Perspectives Graphic Outline

Allows student to select a position and a perspective other than the book's. Maps out needs, concerns, text statements, reader reactions to text statements, and summary position statement from the perspective selected.

Discussion Web

Starts with a yes or no question, then list reasons for yes or no answers, and develops conclusions based on those reasons, which allows for discussion of the validity of the reasons and conclusions regardless of yes or no belief or answer.

Frayer Model

Defines a concept by listing essential characteristics, nonessential characteristics, examples, and nonexamples.

(Continued)

Table 4-5.   Types of Graphic Organizers (*Continued*)

History Change Frame

Shows in a flow chart how people's actions can either solve or create problems, the changes that occurred because of the actions, and the effects of the problems or solutions on people.

Mind Mapping

Maps out new information by defining it and then giving broad characteristics.

Pyramid Diagram

Starts with a topic or concept, then builds information about the topic in layers, becoming increasingly detailed.

Semantic Map

Starts with a central concept in the middle of the page and then connects concepts or content extending out from the center.

Story Map

Addresses who, what, when, why, and how; also gives information about author's theme or intent for discussing information.

Structured Notetaking

Addresses text structure and how information is presented in a text.

(Buehl, 2001)

In Mr. Graham's science classroom, the students have completed readings of the various books on ecosystems that interested them. In a whole-group discussion, Mr. Graham guides them through the various graphic organizers they have learned to use to represent the information they learned. He then has them get in CALCs according to the ecosystem. The small groups get together and discuss what they have learned and what to depict graphically to share with the rest of the class. The discussion in the literature circle centers on how the students can organize the information and what they value and what they find confusing. The students then decide to adopt one type of graphic organizer to use as a group. Table 4-6 shows one group's graphic organizer of the information its members learned about rain forests. They created the organizer in a CALC that concentrated on the key information that each individual brought to the discussion, and together they created a semantic map.

Table 4-6.   Semantic Map of Rain Forests

Animals in the Rain Forest:

Jaguars
Parrots
Red-eyed tree frogs
Sloths
Howler monkeys
Snakes (vipers, pythons, tree snakes)

Needed for:

Medicine
Air to breathe
People's & animals' homes
Plants not found anywhere else
Lumber & other resources to sell

Rain Forests

Located in:

South America
Africa
Puerto Rico
Hawaii
Asia
Central America

Characteristics:

Four stages: emergents, canopy,
  understory, & forest floor
Humid
Lots of plant life
Lots of insects
Usually waterfalls and lots of rain
  (more than 80 Inches a year)

Plants found in the Rain Forest:

Bromeliads (waxy leaves)
Ferns
Hardwood trees
Red passion flowers
Orchids
Herbs

There are times, however, when we want students to create their own graphic organizers to share with the group. Later in a unit it can be useful for students to begin the CALC with each student bringing the beginnings of a graphic organizer. When Lester, Rosa, Shirley, and Margaret met in a circle to revisit wolves in the tundra, they had already created individual organizers. Thus they could discuss the information and the structures of their organizers with each other.

Lester: *I made a pyramid diagram about what I learned about wolves in the tundra. I think it explains pretty well the ways wolves are social animals and how many wolf packs are organized by the jobs they do.*

Shirley: *I like pyramids, too, but for my graphic, I made a history change frame. That way I showed how wolf families, I mean packs, live their lives on the tundra. I started with the birth of one wolf and showed how the wolf grows up, leaves the pack, mates if it is an alpha wolf, and then has babies. I never thought about history as a circle before, but that's sort of how this works.*

Rosa: *You know, you could do a history change frame on that book, uh, Once a Wolf! That's a cool book about the reintroduction of wolves into Yellowstone, but it also gives the history of wolves and how people thought about them and stuff.*

Shirley: *That would be cool to, like, make a larger history of the wolves and then inside the larger graphic, place this circle.*

Lester: *Do you think the history of wolves would be a circle, too, or what?*

Rosa: *Well, the book sort of makes me think that people are thinking that wolves aren't so bad anymore, except some of the ranchers, so maybe that's a circle, too, like a circle of feelings or something.*

Margaret: *Yeah, like people's attitudes are changing or coming back to think of wolves in a better way. But is that a circle? I mean, haven't people always thought wolves were bad?*

Shirley: *I don't know. I could do more work on that if we end up doing an inquiry project on this information. What did you do for a graphic?*

Margaret: *I made a semantic map about wolves living in the tundra. First I had to sort of explain tundra, then I wrote stuff about what wolves ate and how large their territories are, and then finally I put in stuff about their dens and families.*

Lester: *You know, if we put all of our organizers together, we could make a report about wolves, but I think we might need more stuff about the tundra as an ecosystem.*

Rosa: *Yeah, on my organizer, I wanted to think more about the ecosystem and the wolves, so I made a Frayer model. That way I listed the characteristics of the tundra and some examples of stuff that would be there, including wolves, reindeer, and elk. Oh, yeah, and rodents!*

As we listened to these four students discuss their graphic organizers with each other, we became aware of how important it is for students to share their thinking with each other. As their individual personalities allowed them to create different types of organizers, they were also better able to share the different attributes about the information and the way it is represented in their graphics. Because they thought of different elements and ideas from their readings, each of the students became an expert at something while the entire group learned from each individual.

We have also come to realize how important it is to have different ways of representing information available to our students. Because Mr. Graham took the time to teach a number of graphic organizers, his students were better able to fit their needs and interests into an organizer that seemed appropriate to them. By using different organizers, students show us what they are learning and what is important to them. After the CALCs, Mr. Graham was able to assess what his students knew and what he needed to revisit with them.

Conclusion

Familiarizing students with strategies such as think-alouds, "say something," and graphic organizers in the framework of content area literature circles allows students to make use of the power of peer-to-peer learning and teaching. These strategies also help them to frame the key concepts or ideas in ways that allow for more in-depth learning and application of the content under study. They also can become more familiar with expository text structure, how to read it, and how to take advantage of the graphics and figures they see in their texts for their own use. By discussing the big ideas in their readings, students strengthen their summarizing and synthesizing abilities while also engaging in what interests them in their content subjects.

Chapter 5

Attending to Significant Language and Vocabulary in Content Area Literature Circles

I hate learning vocabulary. It is so boring! I mean, all we do is look at words and their definitions and then go on to other words. Half the time I don't get how to use the words we learn. Then they've just gone right out of my head. Why bother?

—Derek, eighth-grade social studies student

There is no argument that the acquisition and application of new vocabulary increases and deepens students' knowledge and understanding of the content within each discipline (Allen, 1999; Smith, 1998). The trick is finding the strategies that engage young people in learning vocabulary without providing the traditional list of words, having the students look them up in a dictionary or the textbook glossary, use them in sentences, memorize their meanings, and regurgitate them on a quiz.

Although learning significant language or vocabulary is often difficult for many middle-level students, another complicating factor involves students who are just learning English. They will need special attention when learning the academic language of a content area. Placing English language learners in content area literature circles (CALCs) with students who are proficient in English is one way to help both groups learn the particular language of evolution, integers, or civil disobedience. Through discussions in CALCs, students not only have the opportunity to acquire and apply the specialized vocabulary or concept language of a particular content area, they also can learn how academic English works.

In this chapter, we define content vocabulary acquisition and application, then discuss the importance of learning the specialized languages of different disciplines. Finally, we describe six specific CALC strategies that encourage and support student learning of content vocabulary.

Helping Students to Learn Content Area Vocabulary

Content vocabulary acquisition and application—learning the particular words, phrases, and conceptual language of a content area—is a necessary part of the study of any discipline. It includes the specialized language—significant words and phrases—that allows for and reinforces the conceptual understandings of individual content areas and is a major part of becoming proficient in that content area.

Traditional methods of vocabulary instruction have grown out of the best of intentions. In the hope that their students will have an easier time comprehending the textbook and other print materials, teachers address difficult or unfamiliar vocabulary in a lesson before the students actually read. Sometimes they ask students to work on vocabulary with a dictionary. The problem with these methods is that students are seldom making use of the vocabulary in any authentic written or spoken context. Learning vocabulary in isolated contexts is not only boring but ineffective (Allen, 1999).

Words need to be understood, spoken, and written in a meaningful context for any lasting vocabulary learning to occur. A meaningful context is often more than a sentence or even a paragraph. For the context to provide sufficient support for learning new content vocabulary, it needs to be within whole, cohesive sections of text as well as used across texts and by the teacher as he or she talks with the students about the concepts they are learning.

Learning Specialized Language

Learning the language used in different disciplines is far more complex than memorizing definitions. Students need to realize that many words have multiple definitions and that the way a word is used in a particular content context will determine its meaning. Providing opportunities in content area literature circles (CALCs) for students to acquire and apply the concept vocabulary as part of their spoken language will also increase their understanding of the content under study. As we teach our students about vocabulary, we also need to consider the following points.

Focus and Connections

When we learn the meaning of a word, we do so by attending to the way it is used in a context. In other words, we focus on the word and its usage. By asking our students to think about how the word is used in a given situation, we increase their abilities to remember and use the word because we have anchored it to something else. We have connected it to other words, ideas, and experiences. For instance, in a unit that focused on reform movements of the late 1800s and early 1900s, Ms. Powers had her sixth-grade social studies students read essays by Booker T. Washington and W.E.B. DuBois. Since these are complex texts for sixth graders to understand, Ms. Powers wanted to deliberately focus her students' attention on the language. First she read aloud the first couple of paragraphs in each essay. Together Ms. Powers and her students selected words or phrases that would be important to an understanding of Washington's and Dubois's ideas, lives, and works. Some of the words they chose were *subservience, prejudice, discrimination, empowerment, patience, respect, equality, equity,* and *diligence.* Working as a whole class, Ms. Powers and her students discussed the significance of these words to the content of the work of these two authors and historical figures. Ms. Powers included these words on her class word wall as well.

Next she asked her students to engage in a CALC focused on a portion of *Up From Slavery,* in which Booker T. Washington discusses his attempt to enter college and the conditions under which the admission personnel would consider his application. Although the students don't yet specifically apply the vocabulary they discussed with Ms. Powers, it is evident that they have acquired some of the underlying concepts and are making important connections to their own lives as well.

Allan: *Here it says how he had to sweep the floor good. If he hadn't swept the floor good would he still be admitted to college?*

Kimberly: *I think he would have had less of a chance because she seemed like she was—pretty, like, doubting of how he was.*

Grant: *They might have given him a second chance. If they gave him—*

Kimberly: *If he could mop good?!?*

Allan: *And if they didn't give him a second chance, he would, like, have to go home. And he didn't have money, so he would have to—*

Grant: *Have to walk—alone, all the way back.*

Kimberly: *That'd be—that'd be stinky.*

Allan: *Stinky, yeah.*

Grant: *'Cause he saved all his money for school and slept on the sidewalk.*

Lisa: *It's sort of sad.*

Kimberly: *Wonder what his mom would have said when he came home, and he's like, "I didn't make it." Would she have been really disappointed, or comforting, or supporting, or what?*

Lisa: *Usually moms are supportive or comforting.*

Allan: *It would have been sad if Booker didn't make it into the Hampton Institute.*

Kimberly: *I know, and he wouldn't have become as good of a Black leader.*

Grant: *I think it's funny that Booker wanted an education so bad. It's just the opposite with some kids today.*

Contrasting Booker T. Washington's desire for education with their own, these students began to think about the difficulty of Washington's life and his pursuit of knowledge. They furthered their discussion to think about the conditions of Blacks under slavery, and why some people wanted to make other people into slaves. Finally, these students expressed the idea that the will to dominate those who are different might be part of the human condition, which they also connected to their lives as young people with authority figures in and out of school. They did so through the use of the language used in the book and the connections they made to it and their readings.

Concept Load

Another point to consider when thinking about vocabulary is concept load. *Concept load* refers to the number of new ideas and new vocabulary introduced to readers at one time or in one chapter. Middle-level students are often not familiar enough with the initial concept of a particular chapter to grasp the other concepts the textbook builds on for more in-depth learning. The concept load of a text may be so dense that students cannot differentiate the particular word or phrase that contains the most pertinent information. They then believe that everything in the passage is important, and they have difficulty discussing the information in any cohesive manner. In this case, the concept load is too heavy for real learning to take place.

Many teachers are like Ms. Saunders. They report that their students cannot distinguish key ideas or concepts from their reading, often due to the language (i.e., significant words and phrases), which increases the density of the concept load. Yet if students discuss what they consider significant words, phrases, and passages in literature circles, those who have difficulty differentiating key points can learn from and with others about what the group believes is important.

For example, in Ms. Saunders's eighth-grade social studies classroom, the students read about adolescent alienation as part of an inquiry on current social problems. When they were asked to find vocabulary words that were new, the word *alienation* was only one of many words on which the students focused. They needed help with these words, because in the context of the article the students still couldn't quite grasp the meaning of the word, and the essay they read didn't explain them. The other words the students selected were *thwarted, pigeonholing, devastating, socioeconomic,* and *clique.*

From these selections, the students formed CALCs and each group tackled a different word. In one of the CALCs that followed the reading of "Tragic Flaws" (Wolk, 2002), four students addressed the word *pigeonholing* along with the connections they made between their own lives and the material they read. The following excerpt is from that CALC:

Seth: *So what does pigeonholing really mean?*

Marcel: *Well, from what I get it means you're sort of put in a little place, like where pigeons live or go or something.*

Letty: *In the article it says something about pigeonholing teenagers into strict and defined groups where they don't get to spend too much time with adults.*

Seth: *So, it would sort of mean to put them in a little box or something where they don't get to say or do what they want.*

Jackson: *Yeah, but is that the point? I mean, my parents aren't going to just let me do whatever I want, and if I said some things to them—no way.*

Marcel: *I think the point in the article is about letting teenagers work with adults instead of ignoring us.*

By talking together, these four students began to grasp the meaning of pigeonholing, not only in the context of the article but as an overall concept. Without understanding the words used in the text, the students initially had a hard time understanding what the author meant by adolescent alienation, a topic of great interest to them. They were witnessing such behaviors in their own school and with their classmates.

By being allowed to select their own vocabulary words, the students talked through some of their meanings and then allowed Ms. Saunders to address the remaining concepts with them. Working together, the class came to the conclusion that by finding their own vocabulary words in a passage, the teacher could teach what she thought was necessary by using the words they wanted to learn.

When we began thinking about the issue of vocabulary learning in CALCs, we realized that working with the words alone would not suffice. When working with Ms. Saunders's students, we decided to follow up their initial CALCs by asking them about the phrases that encapsulated some of those words and the passages that contained those phrases. In the same article that Ms. Saunders used on adolescent alienation, the students selected a number of phrases and sentences that they didn't understand. The following are examples:

- "decoupled the generations"
- "they don't consider that high schools provide fertile soil for such antisocial behavior"
- "affording them virtually no interaction with adults"

Given the opportunity to talk about these phrases with others in CALCs, the students learned some of the specific vocabulary and concepts related to a current social problem that affects young people in middle and high school. They were also able to see how some of this language could be used in their own lives or in other content areas. They were learning how versatile some words are while discovering the specialization of others. Unlocking the meanings of key concept vocabulary, whether it is individual words or phrases, has these effects. From these smaller CALC discussions, teachers can then cover key points that their students may have missed.

As we found with Ms. Powers's students, however, they do address key points and main ideas according to their ideas of what is important. Their prior knowledge of a concept or of content vocabulary is a crucial element in that determination. Thus, when you become frustrated with students' reporting of key points that do not seem to match what you expected, reviewing what students bring to their reading may explain this mismatch. By talking about the reality that different readers will have different perspectives on what is important, you can also talk about the social construction of knowledge (see chapter 1) as well as how a common understanding about what is important can be achieved.

Strategies to Help Students Attend to Language in Content Area Literature Circles

Smith (1988) suggests that all students wish to be part of the "literacy club," but some need a more direct invitation to join. Smith uses the club metaphor to suggest that students often see themselves as outsiders rather than insiders when it comes to a facile use of literacy skills, especially vocabulary acquisition and application. They do not see themselves as a part of the group that "gets it." Inviting students into the science, math, or social science "club" involves scaffolding instruction that addresses the vocabulary used by scientists, mathematicians, historians, or sociologists. Content area literature circles are one way to accomplish this scaffolding.

Student Read-Alouds in Content Area Literature Circles

Learning to use content area texts as a way to build vocabulary must be addressed directly. One way is to adjust students' inner voices to content knowledge reading and learning by reading expository texts aloud. This doesn't mean that all students read at the same time or that they have to read the entire text aloud. The teacher can read aloud short pieces of informational text daily so that the students can hear how language works in expository text structure, or individual students can rehearse a piece to read aloud to their content area literature circle (CALC). In either case, after the reading, the students should discuss the language in their CALCs.

Have students select passages from the text that seem important and read them to the members of their CALC. Once a passage has been read, group members should be invited to discuss the meaning of the passage, their response to it, and how it connects to their lives. Mr. Graham tried this strategy of reading aloud with a group of sixth-grade science students after they read *Once a Wolf: How Wildlife*

Biologists Fought to Bring Back the Gray Wolf (Swinburne & Branden-burg, 2001), a book about the reintroduction of wolves to Yellowstone Park that integrates wildlife biology, ecology, and history. Mr. Gra-ham leads his students through a CALC by asking them to talk about significant words, as well as the phrases and sentences that are con-nected with them and that also contain key points. They had the following discussion:

Lindsey: *The wolf's bad reputation spread throughout Eu-rope. In fairy tales and legends, wolves were evil. Who has not read The Three Little Pigs and Little Red Riding Hood?*

Mr. Graham: *Why do you think she read this part?*

Kristen: *Because when you are little there are more things to be afraid of.*

Amber: *I think she liked that part because in fairy tales, when you're little, you know that things like that couldn't really happen, but it is still possible for wolves to attack you.*

Lindsey: *Actually, I picked it because children are only afraid of wolves because of those stories they hear and what their parents tell them.*

From this short excerpt, we can see that by talking together, these sixth graders are learning to comprehend the text on an interpretive level while also learning the vocabulary that scientists use to describe the world. Later in their discussion, these middle-level girls continued the read-aloud (Table 5-1) and discussion about how wolves are victims to human conditioning, negotiating the language found in the text.

Table 5-1.   Student Read-Alouds

1. Student reads aloud.   Amber: This is what I thought was interesting: "In North America, there is no record of a healthy wild wolf killing or seriously injuring a person. In fact, wolves are shy creatures and avoid people if at all possible."

2. CALC members discuss their responses.
    Lindsey: You chose that because people are afraid of wolves because they think wolves are dangerous. But wolves are really shy.
    Kristen: I think the reason they never attack people is that they really have no reason to. I mean, we haven't done anything to them, and all they want to do is eat, sleep, and care for their pups.
    Amber: I thought it was interesting because it says that wolves are shy creatures and they try to avoid humans, but people still ignore that and hunt them down.

3. Repeat until each member reads a passage and the group discusses it.

By continuing through the book discussing what they considered significant passages, students learn two important elements of content study. The first is how others might find something of value in the information that they themselves did not consider. The second involves the interpretation of the information. By listening to what others think about the information and discussing these ideas together, students gain valuable insights into how knowledge is built and understood in content subjects. They also learn the language that is used by those interested in that particular discipline.

Lindsey, Amber, and Kristen did not select the same passages as they read *Once a Wolf*. They found that by discussing what each one found important or significant, they learned more about wolves. By sharing interpretations with one another, they also learned how to think about the text more deeply, because they were learning from each other about how certain passages can be valuable to each individual.

Word Walls

Another way to help all of your students work on specific vocabulary in content area literature circles (CALCs) is to place a thematic word wall in a location where all students can see it. They should then be encouraged to consult the word wall when they are talking in their CALCs. Table 5-2 gives an example of a thematic word wall.

Table 5-2. Thematic Word Wall

Place a large sheet of butcher paper on a wall or bulletin board with key words from the textbook or the unit materials the class is reading. Words that are used to understand the information from the particular unit are added to the word wall as needed. Students or teacher can add to the list as more content is studied. With each unit, create a new word wall and leave the others on the wall so students will not forget the content they studied before.

The Civil War

Reconstruction	Ulysses S. Grant	Gettysburg
Northern aggression	Secession	Bombardment
Carpetbagger	Munitions	Robert E. Lee
Confederacy	Plantation	Scalliwag
War between the states	Emancipation	Shiloh
Andersonville	Jefferson Davis	Abraham Lincoln
Ironclad	Blockade	Minie ball
Atlanta	Proclamation	Union
Scuffle	Hardtack	Preservation

By deciding in CALCs what words should go on the word wall, all students have the opportunity to talk about the content under study and why particular words should be included as the vocabulary of individual themes. Teachers can eventually have students discuss how words for one theme may also be appropriate for another theme, thus engaging students in understanding how words can be used in multiple contexts. In a small group, students who are just learning English can enjoy what they are learning in terms of both a new language and new information.

Knowledge Charts (KFN)

One strategy we like to use to facilitate students' thinking about concepts and significant words, phrases, or passages is a KFN strategy, which charts the words that students **k**now, are **f**amiliar with, and are **n**ew to them. This chart helps students to learn vocabulary by focusing on their familiarity with the language in a text. If they know the word and its meaning, they do not spend a lot of time thinking about it. If they are familiar with the word but perhaps not its meaning, they focus on connecting its meaning to the content under study or to experiences they have had. If the word is new to them, students spend the most amount of time learning that word and its meaning. Table 5-3 explains how KFN works.

Table 5-3.   KFN

1. Students read the material.
Reading independently, students address their own understanding of the text and identify vocabulary and its usage. They select vocabulary that is of interest and that they believe might be of particular importance to the discipline or content area.
2. Each student creates an individual knowledge chart.
By creating an individual chart, students will have something to offer to the discussion as well as identifying where they have difficulty with the text and its concepts.
3. Each content area literature circle generates a chart.
Through discussion in a CALC, students negotiate the specialized language that the entire group needs to work on and determine who might need help with particular words that others in the group know well.

In Mr. Robine's science class, students generate a knowledge chart as one introductory activity to the space and solar system unit. The chart not only helps the students to see what they know and what they will need to work on, it also helps Mr. Robine to plan his instruction. As Table 5-4 indicates, the students place conceptual language in one of three categories, and Mr. Robine can then check to see what concepts, ideas, or vocabulary he might directly address in a mini-lesson to ensure that all his students can understand what they are reading and studying.

Table 5-4.   Knowledge Chart on Space and the Solar System

Know	Familiar	New
gravity	big bang	asteroids
astronaut	Hubble telescope	meteoroids
planets	comets	aurora borealis
orbit	hydrogen	corona
oxygen	helium	Gaspra
eclipse	lunar	nebula
lifespan	collapse	supernova
galaxy	variables	pulsate

Cubing

The cubing strategy (Table 5-5) gives each individual in a content area literature circle (CALC) the opportunity to think through his or her own perspective on a concept, an idea, a person, or an experience that the group has agreed to investigate. The individuals then meet in CALCs to discuss the thinking that each one has done. Cubing is an excellent strategy to "pack in" information; students not only bring

Table 5-5.   Cubing

The purpose of cubing is to ask each student to think about a word or phrase in six different ways (thus the idea of cubing).

The six ways are as follows:

1. **Describe it**: Give its general characteristics—what it looks like.

2. **Compare it**: Explain how it is similar to or different from something else within the same topical area.

3. **Apply it**: Explain what it is used for and how it is used.

4. **Associate it**: Describe what else it makes you think of and why you make that connection.

5. **Analyze it**: Explain how it is made, and what its component parts are.

6. **Argue for or against it**: Take a stand and list reasons to support or not support it.

One easy example we use to help students understand the six ways to think about an object is through the use of an apple. We bring in different apples (e.g., Granny Smith and Delicious) and then have the students "cube" them.

different perspectives to the discussion, they also bring different definitions and ideas about the concept language.

In this strategy, students meet in CALCs and roll a plastic die to see which prompt they will address. For instance, if the first student rolls the die and gets 3, he or she will be asked to apply (number 3 in Table 5-5) that word, phrase, or concept. With the apple example mentioned in the table, the student might say something about how apples are used in pies or strudels. Once the first person has spoken, a second person rolls the die. If the second student gets the same number as the first student, the second student can either roll the die again to try to get another number or can just share a new idea. Students roll the die until all six numbers have come up. With this strategy, students share their ideas one at a time, with the opportunity to note the differences in their answers. They ask each other questions and make comments. This can be an especially valuable tool for helping students to learn to support their different perspectives with reasoning and with sources.

Through cubing, students more fully investigate the topic they are studying, and they learn to use the language that is necessary for that content area. They also learn to see the multiple ways in which concept language can be viewed.

Groups can also cube in two other ways: (a) They can discuss one particular concept or idea inherent in the reading, or (b) each student can look at a different concept or idea that has emerged from the shared topic or concept.

In whatever way the students and teacher choose to proceed with the cubing strategy, each CALC is expected to complete all six prompts about the concept, idea, experience, or person before beginning a new discussion. The following excerpt is an example of the sharing that happens when students meet to discuss their cubed descriptions:

Michael: *The northern lights remind me of stained glass with light being shown through. What do they remind you guys of?*

Alice: *I think they are like a rainbow, sort of.*

Richard: *Or like a bunch of shooting stars.*

Kelly: *How did you guys define it? Should we use northern lights or Aurora Borealis?*

Richard: *I think we can put both terms—*

Alice: *I said it was lights in the night sky.*

Kelly: *I think we should put that they are colored.*

Michael: *And that they happen because of a natural phenomenon caused by the solar wind.*

Once they have shared as a group, the students can actually create a group cube with agreed-upon information. These can then be shared with the whole class and displayed for individuals and groups to use to see the differences and similarities within or across content concepts.

Pyramid Diagrams

Creating a pyramid diagram (Buehl, 2001) while participating in a content literature discussion is one way for students to think about the relationships in the information they study. A pyramid diagram allows students to analyze a concept from a particular content area and how it connects or relates to other aspects of their reading. A pyramid diagram is an organizer that invites students to start with a larger concept and branch out in a pyramid shape, adding more and more connections or examples on each tier. The information on each tier, however, must fit under the concepts of the tier above. The bottom tier can list examples of the tier directly above it. Table 5-6 is an example of a pyramid using the concept of water in relation to world geography. Ms. Washington's seventh graders created this example as a whole group using the concepts they generated in CALCs from their readings.

Table 5-6.　Pyramid Diagram of Water

Water

Salt　　　Fresh

Large Area Boundaries　　　Flowing　　　Smaller Surface Area

Geographical Bodies of Water

Oceans	Seas	Rivers	Bays	Gulfs	Lakes
Pacific	Black	Mississippi	Fundy	Mexico	Michigan
Atlantic	Japan	Amazon	Qamr	Valencia	Pontchartrain
Indian	Red	Nile	Hudson	Biscay	Geneva
	Mediterranean	Yangtze	Mobile	Cambay	Victoria
	North	Ganges	Mackenzie	Persian	Eyre

Explain the connection among all of these elements.
  They are all bodies of water that we can see on the globe.
  They are big enough to travel by boat.
  They are major waterways.
What geographical bodies of water did you not list, and why?
  Creeks, bogs, swamps, and ponds, because they are too small for our diagram. Also, we couldn't see them on the globe.

Conclusion

As students become more adept at reading informational texts, their ability to use the specialized vocabulary that comes with any content subject will increase. Realizing the importance of concept vocabulary is essential for student learning. In order for your students to willingly come to this realization, you will need to provide engaging ways for them to talk about the language of your content area. Part of being a learner in any content area is becoming an apprentice who is developing an understanding of what it means to think like mathematicians, scientists, historians, sociologists, and economists as well as readers and writers. To help your students become apprentices, you will need to use the strategies discussed in this chapter. Using these strategies will enable your students to join the "content clubs" of the disciplines you teach.

Chapter 6

Addressing Other Points of View in Content Area Literature Circles

[Open-mindedness] includes an active desire to listen to more sides than one; to give heed to facts from whatever source they come; to give full attention to alternative possibilities; to recognize the possibility of error even in the beliefs that are dearest to us.

—John Dewey (1933)

One of our most important tasks as teachers is to guide students on their path to becoming responsible citizens in this increasingly complex world. Students need to understand that there are rarely only one, two, or three ways to think about an issue or a problem. Through reading, inquiring, and discussing, they begin to see that theirs is not the only point of view.

The discussions students have in content area literature circles (CALCs) can play an effective role in helping students to see all sides of an issue or a question. For example, if your students are studying the environment and the theory of global warming, they need to realize that the topic is extremely controversial. During their CALCs, they can discuss their own prior knowledge and views and consider other points of view from the variety of sources they have encountered in their reading. They'll see extremes. At one extreme are the people who are convinced that the human race is headed toward extinction because humans are manipulating and destroying natural habitats and ecosystems. At the other are those who think global warming is a scare tactic created by the environmentalists to inhibit progress. In between, of course, others hold a multitude of perspectives.

It is increasingly important, therefore, that we equip our students with strategies for evaluating an issue or problem from many angles before they make decisions that will affect their lives and the lives of others for years to come. They will also need to understand that "the same text [or set of texts] will have a very different meaning and value to us at different times or under different circumstances" (Rosenblatt, 1983, p. 35).

Helping Students to Consider Other Points of View

Point of view or *perspective* refers to the position from which the reader views, considers, and evaluates the issues, ideas, problems, and questions generated from a reading or a discussion about the reading. Point of view and perspective in content area literature circles (CALCs) are influenced by the relationship between the reader, the text presentation, and the reader's prior knowledge. Readers' perspectives are filtered not only by their purpose for reading, life experiences, and knowledge bases, but also by the qualities of the text: genre, style, voice, and vocabulary (Beach, 1993; Rosenblatt, 1978).

Purpose. The purpose a student has for reading makes a significant difference in how he or she approaches the reading. Therefore, the learning purpose in an academic study is important to a CALC. Purpose helps to keep the CALC focused, because all the group members come with a similar intent. Although points of view will vary, the focus of those views will be the same, minimizing the chance for off-task talk. For example, in order to facilitate the students' understanding of the ways in which informational texts can be constructed around conflict, Holly asked Ms. Washington's seventh-grade social studies students to focus on the conflicts in *Children of the Dust Bowl: The True Story of the School at Weedpatch Camp* (Stanley, 1992) as they read the book in preparation for a CALC.

Life experience and knowledge base. All of our students bring with them a variety of cultural aspects, such as ethnicity, race, class, family structure and tradition, religion, dialect, and gender as well as the spectrum of physical, social-emotional, and academic developmental levels. All of these contribute, along with prior school experiences, to what students have acquired in terms of background knowledge. In the following excerpts from Ms. Mueller's sixth-grade social studies class, we see the influence of students' life experiences and knowledge bases on the kinds of questions they pose in a CALC on a selection entitled "Antonio, a Negro" from *Building a New Land: African Americans in Colonial America* (Haskins & Benson, 2001).

Bernabe: *Where's the Jamestown Colony and the Chesapeake Bay? Are they in Virginia? The person who wrote this thinks we know all this stuff!*

Julianna: *Well, why don't we? We learned it last year!*

Nick: *Yeah, but who remembers? I don't even know where Virginia is now.*

Vanessa: *Well, it says the times were changing and White people were taking advantage of free Blacks. Why would people do that?*

Bernabe: *Prejudice! I mean, they even took his land from his family after he died because he was an alien. What's that supposed to mean? Like he was from outer space or something?*

Julianna: *No! It's like Mexicans who come over the border. They're called illegal aliens. They aren't from here. But if that was true, how did Antonio get over here?*

Genre and style. Authors choose specific genres and styles to communicate their perspectives on an idea, issue, or event. Readers engage with the text to determine the point(s) of view through their own experience and knowledge of the structure of the different genres and styles. Genres can be fiction or nonfiction and can range from such structures as textbooks to picture books, articles, essays, and poetry. As our students use a wider and wider variety of print materials in their content classes, it is important that they discuss the kinds of perspectives that are embedded within different genres and styles. For an in-depth discussion of genre and style in academic materials, see Mooney (2001).

Voice and word choice. All writing has a slant. It is the work of a human being with a particular background and way of thinking. No matter how much authors try in expository texts and textbooks to

Textbook "Facts" Can Be Wrong

In his book, *Lies My Teacher Told Me,* James Loewen (1995) does a great job of debunking the aura of factual accuracy and neutrality in textbooks. For example, in discussing slavery and the causes of racism, he says, "Textbooks stress that Jefferson was a humane master, privately tormented by slavery and opposed to its expansion, not the type to destroy families by selling slaves. In truth, by 1820 Jefferson had become an ardent advocate of the expansion of slavery to the western territories" (p. 140).

appear purely factual, they do take a perspective. For example, a textbook may have the air of accuracy due to the author's use of words like *undisputed* and phrases like "agreed upon by scientists the world over." Rather than relying on the author or the teacher to tell them whether a given piece of writing is accurate, students need to learn ways to determine this on their own.

Young people often do not realize that even "the facts" do not include all the information that many of us need to understand more completely the situations or conditions people face in their lives. Textbooks give facts that privilege certain understandings and certain peoples. Simply look at a history textbook and count the number of women and people of color who are highlighted in it. Although this is improving, it is still an issue our students need to recognize. We are not suggesting that students shouldn't learn the content of their social studies, mathematics, or science texts. Rather, we find that once young people start to question the content in terms of who or what is left in and who or what is left out, they develop critical literacy skills that help them to determine the authenticity and accuracy of the texts they are reading.

When young people consider multiple perspectives, they are involved in critical thinking. When our students bring multiple points of view—their own and those of authors—to CALCs, they must consider the validity of that view and the motivation or intent behind it. When focusing on multiple perspectives, students also need to identify who the author is and what his or her credentials are for writing the article or book. In CALCs, students delve into these issues, share their confusions and concerns, question the perspective, and figure out collaboratively what perspectives make sense to them.

Often, however, they need guidance from their teacher when first learning how to think critically about their reading. For an example, we will again return to Holly's work with Ms. Mueller's sixth-grade social studies students' reading of "Antonio, a Negro." In this excerpt, we share how Holly modeled her question posing as a critical reader. Holly read the first paragraph:

> The story of Anthony Johnson illustrates the change over time in the position of most colonial blacks. His existence is first recorded in 1621, when a slave known as "Antonio, a Negro" was sold to the English at Jamestown. It is likely that he was familiar with European languages, Christianity, and other aspects of European culture.

As Holly read, she pointed out the following questions:

- Where did Antonio Johnson get his name?
- Why did the author use *Blacks* and *slaves* interchangeably?
- What other conditions played into the lives of Africans in the colonies?
- Why is it assumed that Antonio would be familiar with European customs and languages?
- Why is Antonio called a *Negro* and not *African,* when Whites are called *European*?

Once she finished explaining her questions, Holly asked the students about their questions from the first paragraph of the passage. One sixth grader, Irma, asked about a short phrase that discussed slaves being able to marry slaves. Another student, Bernabe, asked about Antonio's past, how Antonio had earned his freedom, and whether this was always possible for slaves. From these questions and three others, Holly was able to talk about how learning to question makes us realize that we don't know the whole story, and sometimes what the book doesn't report is as important to us as what it does. These sixth graders wanted to know more about the conditions of Antonio and other free Blacks in colonial America, but the book had given them only a taste of what could be known.

The Importance of Encouraging Multiple Perspectives

Students become more open-minded. Our students bring into the classroom a diversity in ethnicity, race, class, religion, dialect, and gender. They also bring in one or more perspectives on any given topic every day. For some, letting go of long-held opinions and conclusions is difficult. However, through wide reading across a variety of texts—and open-minded content area literature circles (CALCs)—they come to embrace a wider worldview as they evaluate knowledge and belief systems. Students' responses in CALCs often include comments such as "I never would have thought of that"; or "This is new to me"; or "I've never seen or heard of that before." They may end up retaining or rejecting a particular stance, but they will have made the decision with more clarity and depth because they've thought critically about it with their peers and teachers.

Students clarify their own beliefs and learn to question each other. By using CALC strategies that focus on understanding multiple perspectives, "Teachers do not empower or disempower anyone. . . . They . . . create the conditions under which people empower themselves, or not" (Ruiz, 1991, p. 223). When our students see each group member's different point of view, they gain exponentially. They see one another as having unique and valuable knowledge and understandings. They gain the courage to question their own, or another student's, perspectives in light of what other group members have to say.

Talking with their peers also helps students to question one another to ensure accuracy. For example, after browsing a set of materials to begin a study of the human body in Mr. Dornan's eighth-grade science class, Stephen, Josh, and Marie had the following exchange about the heart in their CALC:

Stephen: *There are lots of ways to get heart attacks, right?*

Josh: *Yeah, like smoking, and eating bad, no vegetables. I can't stand vegetables.*

Marie: *Well, my dad had a heart attack and the doctor said it was because us kids made him upset.*

Josh: *I don't think you can just give someone a heart attack.*

Stephen: *But can't people be a source of stress that would work on you to give you a heart attack?*

Josh: *I think stress can get you to a heart attack, but lots of people have kids, and not all of them have heart attacks. I have four brothers, and they should give anyone a heart attack if it was true that people do it to each other.*

Marie: *Well, it must be the way we all get on each other, and my dad couldn't take it. My mom pretty much ignores our "stress-inducing behaviors." That's what she calls it.*

Stephen: *Your dad will probably live longer if he ignored you, too!*

Josh: *Man, think about it. If kids could give people heart attacks, teachers wouldn't live very long!*

Marie: *That's true. That doctor must have said something else.*

After this initial CALC, the students delved into the materials more deeply to find out what causes heart attacks. They also investigated across texts to see if their references agreed or not and discussed it in their next CALC.

Our students constantly navigate between what they know and what they have yet to learn and explore. By sharing their expertise, knowledge, and understanding, they can take ownership of their beliefs about the world, their impact on it, and its impact on them.

Students hear many voices—and celebrate them. Students need to know that their ideas are not only heard but also celebrated. They learn that their opinions in CALC conversations provide the whole group with a way of thinking about the content in more depth and more extensively. Thus, they realize that their own contributions add to the knowledge of the entire classroom community.

Students value classmates' opinions and experiences. Even when the focus is on fact-based concepts, it's important for students to understand that everyone comes to learning with his or her own biases—different prior knowledge and understandings about the ways of the world. A classroom community that acknowledges difference as positive for working and growing strives toward mutual admiration and caring among all its members. Through CALCs, students—whether close friends or not—can develop a working relationship that focuses on a variety of perspectives drawn from personal experiences, prior learning, and cultural and social influences, as well as the text.

Strategies for Helping Students to Address Other Points of View

When inviting our students to address or accommodate other points of view, we use three strategies in content area literature circles to introduce this way of thinking. These are described below.

"The Picture Tells My Story"

The first strategy involves the use of pictures that the teacher either finds interesting or believes will initiate discussion. Students are asked to form content area literature circles (CALCs) and discuss one of the pictures in each group. Thus, if there are eight groups, the teacher will need eight photos for the class. Students respond to the pictures individually by writing a short paragraph or essay that addresses some of the following generic questions:

- What's happening and why?
- Who does this involve? What makes you think so?
- Where is this taking place?
- What is going to happen next?
- How do you feel about the content of this "text"?
- Why do you think this photograph was taken?

Once the students have written their paragraphs or essays, they then discuss their responses with their CALC. As part of the criteria for this strategy, students are asked to justify their reasoning *in relation to the content under study,* which is one reason this is such an exciting strategy to use in content areas like science, math, and social studies. Once students start to share, they find that they have different ideas about what the photograph is "saying." Because the photos and the students' responses are about the content under study, they begin to realize that there are many ways to view academic content. We call this strategy "the picture tells my story" because students will realize what assumptions they bring to any text, and that in many ways their ideas, responses, and understandings of the content are connected to these assumptions as well as to their life experiences and academic background.

We find many of our picture prompts in magazines such as *Time* or *Life,* but we've also used advertisements, newspaper photos, art essays, sports magazines, and teen magazines to prompt discussion. We usually mount our selections on a piece of construction paper and laminate them so we can use them again.

Once students begin to understand the multiple perspectives brought to their CALCs, we explain how many perspectives could be represented in the class (one per person in the room), and then we explain that even in the world of science, math, or social studies, there are many different theories or perspectives about the events that have happened in those fields.

"Save the Last Word for Me"

"Save the last word for me" is a strategy that helps students to realize that there is more than one interpretation of a text (Short et al., 1996). Students share their multiple interpretations of a piece of writing in content area literature circles (CALCs), which can take the form of comments, examples, or questions, and allows the students to state their views and opinions of the content under discussion. The strategy proceeds as follows:

1. Students read the same text selection independently.

2. As they read, they write on one side of 3 x 5 index cards phrases, sentences, or segments of the text that catch their attention. On the other side of each card, they write what they want to say about that particular segment.

3. Students meet in CALCs of three members each, and one of the members starts the process by reading the significant passage, phrase, or sentence to the other members. They do not yet read what they want to say about the passage.

4. The other members of the literature circle then respond to that passage or segment.

5. The student who read the quote has the last word about the passage.

6. The next member of the CALC then selects a quote from the text, and the cycle continues until all members have shared or they run out of cards or time.

As part of "save the last word for me," we ask students to consider the following guidelines to help them become more critical thinkers, listeners, discussants, and readers while also remaining respectful to other perspectives.

Sharing without critique. Each member of the CALC takes a turn saying something about how he or she connects the information that has been shared. Students share their thinking without critique.

Questioning ideas. Once all have shared about a particular passage, students are encouraged to question their perspectives and to seek support for their thinking for their next meeting.

Confirming and rejecting. When the group comes together for another session, each student has had a chance to revisit some of the materials and has found supporting information and has confirmed or rejected some of his or her initial ideas. Learning to support ideas is an essential aspect of being a fully educated person in our society, and CALCs give students the practice they need to try out their ideas and support them. As we listen to our students talk, we often notice that students do more than simply list their ideas. They challenge, and are challenged by, others. Therefore, the CALCs move into more complex discussions in which students can respond to each other's questions with specific support from their reading or supplemental materials. Eventually, content discussions can become venues for students to theorize about a topic based on the materials they read. Students become more adept at logical thinking and reasoning as well as supporting their opinions with confidence.

"Meeting of the Minds"

The "meeting of the minds" strategy expands students' thinking so they can see things from the perspective of others and can synthesize the information they've been learning. In this strategy, students adopt either (a) the persona of the author of a particular text, or (b) the persona of an animal, a thing, a place, a person, or a concept that is discussed in the text.

Students then meet in content area literature circles (CALCs) as these different personas and focus on the different perspectives that each of the "minds" brings to the concept or topic under study. This type of discussion is an excellent way for students to compare and contrast information in a fun and engaging way while also considering the different perspectives that can be taken in regard to a concept, an idea, or an experience. Once they have discussed from their perspectives, students can discuss as a group the way they might want to present the information to the rest of the class. This last step is optional, but again, it is a fun and engaging way to learn content.

Ms. Mueller's social studies class used this strategy as part of its study of women of accomplishment. (For this same strategy, Mr. Dornan's students adopted different body systems.) Ms. Mueller's students divided into groups of four for their reading and their CALCs. One student in each group read a different book from the following list:

> *The Riches of Osceola McCarty* (Coleman, 1998)
>
> *Oseola: Memories of a Sharecropper's Daughter* (Govenar, 2000)
>
> *Fly High!: The Story of Bessie Coleman* (Borden & Kroeger, 2001)
>
> *Just Passing Through: The Story of Sojourner Truth* (Rockwell, 2000)

We share excerpts from one of Ms. Mueller's classes to show how "meeting of the minds" can work. Each student studying women of accomplishment adopted the persona—and perspectives of—the woman about whom he or she studied. Each became an "expert" on that persona and became her advocate in the following discussions. It's important for the members of each group to decide what their personas are expected to discuss. The sixth graders studying women focused on each persona's accomplishments and stumbling blocks.

To begin the discussion, the students first took turns sharing who they were and one or two major attributes of their personas:

Vanessa: *Hello. Glad to meet you all. My name is Osceola Mays, and life for me was hard. I was a Black child growing up as a sharecropper's daughter.*

Dannie: *What's a sharecropper?*

Vanessa: *That's where my daddy worked the land and made a crop, but then had to share with the White man who owned the land.*

LaToya: *That sounds like slavery, which is how I lived my life before Lincoln saved us. My name is Sojourner Truth and I let people know I was equal to White women by asking the big question "Ain't I a woman?" That got people all stirred up.*

Dannie: *I should think so. I'm Bessie Coleman, and I got people stirred up in Texas and in other places when I wanted to be a pilot. They didn't think women should do that, but I think they were also wondering if a Black woman could do that. I think it was because it was in 1920, I had to go to France to learn how to fly.*

LaToya: *And who are you, Ma'am?*

Michelle: *Well, that's funny. My name is Osceola, too, but my last name is McCarty. I lived a hard life, too, but toward the end of it, I gave $150,000 to the University of Southern Mississippi so that other young people could stay in school. I wanted to stay in school when I was young, but I couldn't because we were so poor.*

Dannie: *It's funny how I was able to go to university, but I still couldn't do what I wanted, and you couldn't even go to school.*

Vanessa: *Goodness! I worked hard like you, too, Osceola! I did laundry and worked in White people's homes. I also came from Texas, like you, Bessie! I didn't get to go to school, but with my storytelling, I did go to France. And my parents were slaves, like you, Sojourner. We have a lot in common, I think.*

LaToya: *I didn't get to go to school, either. But I think I am an important person in history.*

Vanessa: *I may not be important for history, but because I told my stories [as a sharecropper's daughter], I added to history.*

Michelle: *I don't think I am important in history, but I am hoping that the money I gave to the university will let some other young person do something important.*

Dannie: *Well, lots of people don't know about me, but I made history. We are all important Black women!*

Much of what these four girls discussed came directly from their readings. Their assignment was to make connections to each other and to see how the lives of the four women they studied could be compared.

Once the groups have discussed their personas, we ask each group member to jot down notes from the discussion. This will often cause students to go back to their book to clarify any questions and add information. We have found that it is worth tape-recording these sessions so that both you and your students can review what was discussed. Using the notes, the group then meets and organizes its information into paragraphs and creates written documentation of its work. Students can use their discussions to write a script that they perform for the other groups in the class, for groups of younger students, or for parents.

Conclusion

The ways in which we as teachers set up content area literature circles can have a profound influence on broadening our students' abilities to open up and take a more empathetic stance toward others whose backgrounds and opinions are vastly different from their own. Learning how to agree to disagree is an important skill, not only for school but for life in a democracy. The multiple-perspectives focus helps our students to learn how knowledge about the world is generated and that all of it comes with some human bias and perspective. The protocols a scientist determines to use will make a difference in the outcomes of his experiments. The people a historian interviews or the primary documents she examines will change her theories about the causes and effects of certain events.

Understanding and celebrating multiple perspectives is critical to moving toward a society that is free from all of its negative biases or "isms"—racism, sexism, classism, ageism, ethnocentrism. Students develop the kind of open-mindedness that Dewey called for when he said, "It includes an active desire to . . . give full attention to alternative possibilities."

Chapter 7

Question and Problem Posing in Content Area Literature Circles

Problem and question posing brings young people to the source of knowledge and to the source of knowledge—other people. When we want our students to think like historians, sociologists, and economists in social studies classes, mathematicians in math class, scientists in science class, and writers in language arts classes, we must involve them in how knowledge is created and known, and types of questions and problems that come with particular disciplines. Content area literature circles (CALCs), in which questions are asked and problems are posed, allow students to become involved in the process of coming to know in content disciplines. If young people are not invited to ask questions and pose problems about content acquisition, they may never connect to content knowledge in any real way. We need to demonstrate to them and apprentice them in the asking of questions that drive our particular content areas.

In this chapter, we will talk about the ways in which CALCs facilitate students' use of question and problem posing to deepen comprehension, knowledge acquisition, and knowledge application. We explore the following:

- Creating question and problem posers
- A creative problem-solving model
- The importance of question and problem posing

- Strategies for initiating question and problem posing
- Working with students who struggle

Creating Question and Problem Posers

Question and problem posing is an invitation for middle-level students to be the creators of knowledge and to voice what they might wonder about in the texts they are reading. Question posing involves students asking questions that may be quite literal or questions that address critical literacy such as author intent, reasons for the writing, and who or what is considered more important in the text. For instance, questions that address evolution in a more literal way might include what is evolution, how did the theory develop, and what species are involved? More critical questions could include a discussion of what the difference is between theory and hypothesis in scientific versus lay terminology.

Levels of Comprehension

Literal Level: Answers are found right in the passage or text.

Interpretive Level: Answers come from what the author implied, so answers need support from the text.

Application Level: Answers come from a combination of the text and the reader's experience to express an opinion or a new idea, so answers need to be explained.

Problem posing involves acknowledging that problems or tensions exist either within or because of events, situations, behaviors, or attitudes. For instance, middle-level students may innately know that lockers are too small for their books, coats, umbrellas, and the other things they bring to school, but they don't ever bring the problem to the attention of a larger public arena where solutions might be discussed. Sometimes we might see an event such as a birthday celebration for an elderly relative as something wonderful, but we might not perceive that the person honored does not like loud noises. Problem posing would take into account that problems could exist.

We want students to pose questions and problems because it leads to deeper, more creative and constructive thinking. In the 21st century, such thinking is certainly needed. Students need, however, a way to think about problems and solutions. The creative problem-solving model helps middle-level students to organize their thinking.

The Creative Problem-Solving Model

The creative problem-solving model provides students with the following step-by-step process to use to take information they have read, flesh out a problem, and work toward a solution:

1. Identify challenges in the situation.
2. Determine an underlying problem.
3. Produce solution ideas to the underlying problem.
4. Generate and select criteria to evaluate solution ideas.
5. Apply criteria to solution ideas.
6. Develop an action plan.

The first two steps, identifying challenges and determining an underlying problem, are essential, as they encourage students to think about and begin to understand the relationship between problem posing and problem solving in their classrooms or their world. In completing the first two steps, students realize that identifying and determining a problem is the beginning of the search for the solution.

To pose a problem, however, requires the ability to pose questions. Holly asked seventh-grade students to work through the problem-solving process as part of her teaching of plot. She used problem solving to address the types of conflict found in most pieces of Western literature. She found that students had difficulty identifying the conflict or problem element in a piece of writing, whether the writing was narrative or expository. When the students did identify some of the superficial problems in a text, they still had difficulty ascertaining if these problems were related to a deeper or more underlying problem. Lacking the skill of problem and question posing often hindered her students from completely understanding or appreciating the information they read. Learning to ask questions from the books they were reading, and then to share their questions with each other in content area literature circles, the students began to see how problems exist and that problems are not a simple matter of identification. As they discussed the reasons behind their questions, they began to realize that problems exist in relation to who is involved and who may be affected by the problems. For instance, many communities are faced with the dilemma of where to place their jails or their garbage dumps. Although some solutions might please one group of citizens, a group that lives closer to the proposed sites might object. When middle-level students begin to think about problems and their solutions, they find that not all solutions are appropriate or pleasing to all people.

The Benefits of
Question and Problem Posing

In content area literature circles (CALCs), students can initiate, pose, and answer their own questions and those of others. They learn to do the following:

- Theorize about the world
- Discuss their questions and hypothesize answers
- Understand how important question and problem posing is for literate behavior and for comprehending all kinds of texts
- Think beyond the superficial and process the information more deeply
- Connect how the material informs their lives and the lives of others
- Recognize when the material may assume knowledge that they don't understand
- Become more active in the comprehension and questioning of the knowledge they are learning

Additional benefits of question and problem posing are discussed below.

Questions improve comprehension. By asking questions, students improve their reading comprehension (Keene & Zimmerman, 1997). They are also pushed to consider text structure, author intent, and their own connections to the content under study. They pose questions about their reading process, their familiarity with a particular text structure, and their understanding of the content or concepts about which they are reading. Through question posing, students learn to "recognize and listen to the dissonance in [their] heads," which is one way we have asked students to begin addressing the questions that produce more active meaning making in their reading and more engaged learning of content.

The teachers we worked with invited students to question one another in their CALCs as part of an inquiry curriculum. Through the use of CALCs, students were able to discover and discuss the information they still needed to know and thus develop questions around the unknown. From these questions, students could decide if they needed the information for presenting their inquiry projects, and if the questions became stimulating enough, students knew they could be researched during "Friday free times." One teacher we worked with allowed her students to work on their own questions on Fridays when she created free time. Her students understood that this was not a time to do what they liked, but rather a time to freely find answers to some of the questions they had generated throughout the week that still had them wondering about an answer.

Questioning creates better problem solvers and thinkers. Question posing leads students to more problem posing and, hence, improves problem solving and involves challenging the information provided in content texts that present "the facts." As we mentioned in chapter 1, young people often fail to realize that "the facts" do not include all the information that they need to understand fully the situations or conditions people face in their lives. Regardless of the text, there is bias because of what is selected to be included and what is not considered important enough to be included. Critical thinking skills will enable students to judge the content of what they are reading.

In Table 7-1, we address some of the thinking skills that students develop by becoming question and problem posers in CALCs. CALCs

Table 7-1.   Thinking Skills for Question Posing

Analogical Reasoning: Identifying how one set of concepts is similar to another set of concepts. Example: How is a human skeleton like the frame of a house?

Extrapolation: Determining how a generalized pattern from one piece of information can fit information from another context. Example: What can be learned about our democratic system of government by understanding the systems of the body?

Evaluation of Evidence: Determining whether a claim can be supported or not. Example: How do we know that toxic pollution causes human illnesses?

Examination of Value: Determining the value of specific information, analyzing the assumptions underlying the information and its value, and identifying other assumptions that would challenge that value. Example: Whose perspective on smoking is most believable, tobacco companies; or a lung cancer victim? What does each perspective have at stake? Why?

Decision Making: Systematically selecting from a variety of alternatives. Example: How should I spend my babysitting money?

Elaboration: Inferring information that is not directly stated. Example: How does knowing the fat content of french fries impact my health?

Invention: Creating a new procedure to solve problems or answer questions. Example: How can we increase the number of forests and still have room for people to live?

are especially important in question and problem posing because every person benefits from the additional input that his or her peers can give.

Questioning creates critical thinkers. Because we believe that all texts have a subjective perspective no matter how objective authors try to make them, students should be able to ask pertinent questions about the objectivity of any account, any procedure, or any event about which they read. Learning how to ask such questions, however, can be difficult. Students can learn to ask critical questions about power, and its connection to expository texts written in an objective and authoritative way, by working in CALCs that address the concepts of power and social capital. By *social capital* we refer to Gee's (1996) idea of "goods." Gee asserts that "by 'goods' I mean anything that the people in the society generally believe are beneficial to have or harmful not to have, whether this be life, space, time, 'good' schools, 'good' jobs, wealth, status, power, control, or whatever" (p. 21).

By allowing students to work through issues of power and authority within the texts they use to learn content knowledge, teachers demonstrate not only how knowledge changes but also how knowledge is situated to present information in ways that may not be beneficial for all peoples. For instance, presenting westward expansion and Manifest Destiny without looking at the displacement of American Indians allows the myth of progress as a positive movement for all peoples to persist. Asking questions about who did not benefit from such progress allows young people to see alternative perspectives on historical, scientific, and mathematical "advancements." From discussions that expect students to view information from multiple perspectives, students begin to develop a broader and deeper understanding of the content studied.

Thus, critical literacy includes becoming aware of the power relationships within the content of the text (Comber & Simpson, 2001) and identifying the cultures that create them. It also includes learning to recognize those relationships before taking "the facts" at face value. For example, it is important for our students to recognize that in many textbooks, Christopher Columbus is celebrated while the consequences of his exploration and discovery on the Taino peoples are mostly ignored. This is another reason that using trade books along with the textbook, or using text sets of materials, is beneficial. Following is a list of elements of critical literacy that middle-level students can address in their CALCs:

- Questioning the stance of the author
- Asking what information is missing
- Wondering whom the information benefits and whom it doesn't
- Asking who is telling the story about whom
- Asking why this information is important and under what circumstances
- Questioning the tone of the passage
- Challenging your stance as reader
- Asking how the information would change if someone from another cultural or ethnic group wrote about the topic
- Questioning the use of particular words or language in the text
- Asking who gets to tell the story and why
- Questioning the relationships of power within the text (author to audience, subject to subject, group to group)

CALCs create the opportunity for students to realize how knowledge is actually constructed—through social situations where people can think and talk together. Through the process of talking about how they created the questions they share in CALCs, they become more engaged with each other, thus learning that people approach the content from different perspectives. In essence, they learn one of the most important comprehension strategies from their peers—how to question effectively so they can appreciate the information that they are learning and how this information is important to their lives and the lives of others.

Scaffolding Question Posing

I began to realize that asking tough questions and providing a venue for conversation about them is, perhaps, our most important work.

—Ellin Oliver Keene (1997)

Holly invited her students to think about the ways in which many literary and informational texts are constructed around conflict. She asked her students to think about one of the conflicts in *Hatchet* (Paulsen, 1988), and then to come up with questions that might bring to light the problems they saw within the text. Because her students found this a difficult endeavor, Holly used a picture book that centered on a problem about garbage as a demonstration tool.

Using the picture book *Katherine and the Garbage Dump* (Morris, 1992), Holly asked her students to look for problems as she read to them aloud. This book presents a young girl who finds a piece of garbage thrown in her sandbox one day. Soon other neighbors are throwing their trash not only in her sandbox but also in her yard, which then becomes overflowing with garbage. Katherine attempts to find a solution to this problem but encounters a number of problems and attitudes along the way. Because the text is filled with so many problems, it makes for a good way to introduce problem posing to middle-level students.

After attempting to read the entire story before asking students for feedback, Holly realized that looking for conflict in the situation established by the book was difficult for her students because there were so many problems that had the potential to be identified or posed. Rereading the story, Holly stopped at particular places where she believed problems existed and then asked, "Is there a problem here? If so, what is it?" The students began to list the problems they identified, and once the class had finished reading the book, individual students went to the blackboard and listed the problems they saw in the text. Some of their problems included the following:

- The garbage in Katherine's yard
- The neighbors' beliefs that her yard was a garbage dump
- That city hall didn't want to listen to Katherine
- That Katherine was too young to do anything
- That Katherine couldn't clean up her yard fast enough so people wouldn't think it was a dump

From that list, students then formed CALCs and discussed what they saw as underlying problems that resulted in situations they encountered in the story. They did this by asking themselves the following questions:

- What is the underlying problem?
- What makes it a problem?
- Is it a problem for everyone in the situation?
- Whose problem is it?
- What makes it this person's (or group's) problem?
- What other issues are involved in this problem?
- Are there other people or events causing the problem?

Once the students were able to identify problems, they were able to ask questions that would help them to determine an underlying condition, attitude, or situation. From this, other questions arose that addressed the use of garbage, the excessive packaging of products, and the issue of garbage collecting and its social capital in our society. By learning to pose problems from situations and ask questions about those problems, Holly's students were able to transfer the process of problem and question posing to their own lives. We believe that such processing allowed them to better comprehend the world with greater depth and insight. They learned that some of the issues that did not involve them directly as young people could become important to them eventually. For instance, the students realized that one day they might be faced with a civic element such as a garbage dump or detention center in their neighborhoods and that they may not have a voice in whether it should be placed there or not. They also began to think about the issues of stereotyping against young people because they are young, and that when they are able to drive there might be a prejudice against them.

Taking this idea of problem posing and learning how to ask questions to identify problems either in the account they read or the conditions they read about, Holly worked with Ms. Mueller's sixth-grade students on a short passage about African Americans in colonial America. The students read a short excerpt from the book *Building a New Land: African Americans in Colonial America* (Haskins & Benson, 2001), entitled "Antonio, a Negro," which highlighted the "changes over time in the position of most colonial blacks" (see excerpt in chapter 1). Modeling how she poses questions as a critical reader, Holly read the first paragraph, which introduces Antonio and his circumstances to the reader. She pointed out places where she had questions. (Her questions and the students' discussion are described in chapter 6.)

The students read the rest of the three-page passage and wrote down their questions in their social studies journal. The reading took them about 10 minutes, and then the students volunteered their questions while Holly and Ms. Mueller wrote them on the board. After generating more than 20 questions, the students were invited to theorize about the answers to their own questions as a class. Vanessa, anxious to "talk about the answers to some of these questions," wondered if they could start to talk about their ideas. Taking Vanessa's request as an entry point, Ms. Mueller's students got into their CALCs.

Using some of the information from the passage along with their prior knowledge of Black history, the students made inferences, speculated about the world of the past, and made observations about their present experiences. Later, Ms. Mueller encouraged them to use the Internet, their textbooks, and classroom encyclopedias to find out more about slavery, how the laws changed, and the types of crops planted in Virginia in the 1600s. Several of her students went to the library to find other sources on Black-American history, while others wondered what was happening in Texas at that time. Of the four students whom we followed with audiotape (see chapter 1), Vanessa and Bernabe went to find out more about slavery, whereas Nick checked to see where Virginia was on a classroom globe. Julianna, curious about what was happening in Texas, asked Ms. Mueller to borrow a Texas history book so she could find out more.

From this demonstration, whole-class question posing, and the CALC, Ms. Mueller's students were better prepared to work in future CALCs with questions they had from a text. They also found out that to have questions is an aspect of being a good reader, whereas before they had thought that by asking questions they were showing what they didn't know. Now they understood that asking questions may actually show them to be more careful and critical readers.

Questions to Pose in Content Area Literature Circles

> *The questions were hard sometimes. We really had to think on details and on a wide spread (broad way). It is something I am not used to doing. . . . You (Holly) ask a question and then it's, "Well, why did you think that and how did you get to this?" Normally, [teachers] ask the question and then it's, "Okay, good," and then they move on and it's, like, in the whole class.*
>
> —Rebecca, age 12

There are a number of different types of questions that are appropriate for content area literature circles (CALCs) that will help students to understand text structure as well as develop students' reasoning skills for thinking about content knowledge. By learning to ask particular types of questions that allow for different ways of thinking or viewing the situations they read about or study, middle-level students increase their understanding of the topic and how that topic may be related to other information.

Through question posing, students increase their acquisition of content knowledge while also increasing their ability to reason. They also pose questions as part of their metacognitive awareness while reading a text. Yet it often takes thinking with others to hone those skills, and CALCs create such a venue. The following list of generic questions that we generated for use with middle-level students combines critical thinking and metacognitive awareness skills so that students will have better insight into what they are reading, how they are reading the information, and what they may need to understand the information better:

- What more could I know about this information?
- What other ways could the author present this information?
- How does this information connect to my life? To other information I've read?
- How do I feel about this information?
- Where could I learn more about this topic?
- How am I confused about this topic?

Strategies for Encouraging Question and Problem Posing

Middle-level content textbooks are hard for many students to understand. Yet students are expected to comprehend the information so that learning can take place. For comprehension to occur, students must "actively construct relationships between the information in the text and their background knowledge" (Reutzel & Cooter, 1996, p. 207). Through talk in content area literature circles, students can be actively engaged in making meaning, especially when their teachers scaffold this engagement by using guiding questions that will help students to learn how to pose questions and then discuss those questions with others. Yet we have found that learning to ask questions can be a difficult endeavor for many middle-level students. The teachers we have worked with use a number of strategies over several weeks to help their students learn how to ask questions that go beyond the literal comprehension of a text. We discuss three of these strategies below.

Question-Answer-Relationship

One way for students to gain critical thinking skills through discussion in their content area literature circles (CALCs) is to examine their questions, their answers, and the relationships between them. By modifying the Question-Answer Relationship (QAR) strategy (Raphael, 1986), teachers create opportunities for middle-level students to focus on how questions and answers are connected as well as to realize that not all the information they might want to know is contained in the text. They also recognize that not all questions have a literal answer; there are questions that demand interpretation or application. We usually discuss the levels of comprehension with our students so they will understand that the questions asked may require them to think more deeply about the content. Thus they will comprehend the content on multiple levels.

Some answers are inferred from what we already know and can add to what the material contains, and at other times we theorize based on our knowledge of the content and of the world. QARs inform middle-level readers about what they need to do to answer a question. Do they have to look in the text? Do they need to make an inference? Do they have to answer the question on their own without direct information from the text? By learning to ask questions about situations in a text, students find that not all the questions they have are answered through their reading, but may indeed come from connections they are making between the reading and their background knowledge.

Table 7-2 explains the QAR strategy. We use it in CALCs to have students discuss where they found their answers so that they are not only aware of what they did to find the answer to some of the questions we may ask of them as a group, but so that each group

Table 7-2.   QAR Procedure

1. *"Right There":* Students find the words that created the question in the actual text. The sentence that contains the wording is the sentence that will answer the question. The answer is "right there" in the text.

2. *"Think and Search":* The question is answered directly in the text, but in more than one sentence. The reader needs to "think and search," or use the information from several sentences to answer the question.

3. *"On My Own":* These types of questions can be answered from the reader's prior knowledge.

4. *"Writer and Me":* Readers infer answers by combining their prior knowledge and the information found in the text.

Roe, Stoodt, & Burns (2001)

member can benefit from the thinking of others. It is through inter-actions with others in a more social situation that students can be-gin to accommodate a variety of ways of thinking, complete assignments, and understand how we come to find the answers to questions that are not literally found in the text.

In Ms. Mueller's social studies class, we demonstrated how we approach questions about content by using the QAR strategy with the book *Maria Paints the Hills* (Mora, 2002). This short picture book is a biography of Santa Fe artist Maria Hesch, who painted in the primitive style similar to Grandma Moses. The students were placed in CALCs and then Ms. Mueller read the book aloud to them. Before reading, however, she placed the QAR types on an overhead and asked the students to consider questions as they listened. Once she fin-ished the read-aloud, Ms. Mueller asked students to ask each other questions about the book and to think about what kinds of questions they asked in relation to QAR. The following is a brief interchange about one question addressed in one of her sixth-grade CALCs:

Alicia: *Why do you think the author started the book that way?*

Beatriz: *Maybe to get us kids involved because she thought we might like kites, too.*

Rosemary: *Okay, okay! What kind of a question was that? What do we need to do to answer that kind of question?*

Beatriz: *Well, the answer isn't in the book, and I think we are kind of guessing, so maybe it's an "on my own" kind of question. But, really, we sort of did it together be-cause I probably wouldn't even think about this if Alicia didn't asked me.*

Portia: *My answer wouldn't be the same as yours to that ques-tion [about why the book started that way], but I think it has to be an "on your own" question because the author doesn't give any hints about the answer, ei-ther. And we could "think and search," but I still don't think you would find the answer.*

From this brief exchange, we found that sixth graders can distin-guish and discuss the kinds of questions they ask and the kind of thinking it takes to answer the typical questions they might ask about a book or an author. We wondered, however, if this kind of analysis of questions was engaging to young people, and Alicia explained that "thinking about the questions and what kind they are is kind of fun. It makes me think more than if we were all just talking and asking questions." We believe that discussing the kinds of questions they ask and what thinking it will take to answer those questions is enjoyable. It also empowers students because it makes them feel knowledgeable. The QAR strategy is an excellent way to invite middle-level students into analytical thinking, a vital skill in the 21st century.

In addition, using a QAR is a beginning step for helping students to realize that answers are not always in a text but are often the result of the combination of text and reader knowledge. With consistent usage, students become more adept at seeing the connections between questions and answers that can be examined in a very direct and obvious manner. Such understanding will help students to better comprehend the content they read. Students will also come to realize what kind of knowledge they will need to answer the question they are being asked. We suggest, however, that students should also explore beyond the obvious relationships examined by a QAR and look at how readers' values or belief systems influence their thinking about the questions they are asked or may ask themselves, as well as the answers they construct to those questions.

The W of KWL

One way to support content learning in a content area literature circle (CALC) is through a modified "what I want to learn" (W) of the "What I know, what I want to learn, and what I learned" (KWL) strategy (Ogle, 1986). Ms. Mueller used a modified W with her sixth-grade students to help them become better inquirers of the knowledge they are learning. The following vignette illustrates how Ms. Mueller worked with her students to help them rethink the KWL with which they were familiar. The students then worked in CALCs to develop questions that could not only drive their reading and studying but also show them how questions are a continuous part of the learning process.

Creating a form to use with the students, Holly and Ms. Mueller thought about how to keep students "wondering" as they read. First, Ms. Mueller asks the students questions to access their prior knowledge. By doing this, she is able to discover what the students already know (the K of KWL). Making a list of what they know, she then asks the students to think about what they want to know (the W of KWL). This is the first part of the Wondering As We Read form (Appendix C) that students fill out individually. Students then browse their textbooks as well as the books Ms. Mueller has selected that cover American explorers. After their initial browsing of 10–15 minutes, students select several passages to read independently.

With their wondering sheets in hand, students read and produce a number of questions or wonderings that are of interest to them individually. Ms. Mueller then asks her students to decide on two questions or wonderings that they would like to work through or develop with others in CALCs, and students bring their questions and wonderings to the circles. The following discussion involves three students from Ms. Mueller's class who were studying the explorers who came to the Americas:

> **Destany:** *I wonder why the explorers were looking for cities of gold. Where did they get those ideas? I mean some of the explorers made sense 'cause they were looking for rivers and stuff.*
>
> **Sally:** *I guess some people had lots of gold and, you know, put gold on their buildings.*
>
> **Isaac:** *Sometimes I think it's funny that gold means so much. Why not peanuts?*
>
> **Sally:** *'Cause peanuts are cheap!*
>
> **Isaac:** *You know, I wonder why people explored, anyway. Why didn't people just stay where they were? Then they wouldn't have bothered other people and killed so much stuff, like animals and the rain forest.*
>
> **Destany:** *And Indians! Don't you wonder what it would have been like to be the first colonists, or what the meetings between the Indians and White people would have been like?*
>
> **Sally:** *I'm glad I didn't have to live back then. Think about stuff like [no] electricity and toilets. Yuck!*
>
> **Isaac:** *Yeah, and computers. No computers or game boy or anything. Man, what did those people do all day?!*
>
> **Destany:** *They worked! Even the little kids. We would be planting cotton or something and feeding cows and pigs!*
>
> **Isaac:** *I would have definitely been an explorer, then! I would be on a ship sailing all over the place.*
>
> **Sally:** *Did you read about what women could do? Get married or be a nun!*
>
> **Destany:** *But that one lady still became a poet. She was one of my questions: "Where can I find the poems of Juana Ines de la Cruz?"*
>
> **Sally:** *She asked critical questions about how the people ruled and who got to dominate and stuff, like we're supposed to do. We could study her!*

Through their wonderings, the students can more fully develop questions or problems in CALCs and then proceed to study as they work in their content classrooms.

A modification we consider when teaching our students about the W of KWL involves another W: Why? Asking our students to consider why they want to learn something opens up discussions about interest, self-efficacy, and affect in learning. We believe that middle-level students can discuss their confidence about learning as well as perhaps rethinking why they do or don't like something. We know that interest in a subject will improve reading comprehension, and if our students don't like a particular content or topic within a content area, it can be difficult to teach them. By asking why, students can begin to think about the intention and purpose of learning along with how they might change their affect so that they might enjoy learning something in which they originally had no interest.

Modified ReQuest Procedure

Another strategy that we developed to scaffold Ms. Mueller's students' question posing about world history was to modify the reciprocal questioning procedure called ReQuest (Manzo, 1969). Most often, ReQuest is used for students who are having difficulty attending to the text at a very basic level. Although learning to ask questions about the content as they read helps students to understand the message of the text, it does not push them to question how the text was written and for whom or for what purposes beyond the basic knowledge that they often accept uncritically. The typical ReQuest procedure highlights a literal comprehension level that we wanted to extend so students could move toward a more critical stance that they can readily use in content area literature circle (CALC) discussions.

1. Students and teacher read a selection of the textbook silently. (The teacher determines the length of the selection based on the comprehension abilities of the readers involved.)

2. The students ask the teacher questions about the material.

3. The teacher answers the questions and then changes roles with the students by asking questions about the material.

4. Students and teachers read another selection from the textbook and repeat steps 2 and 3.

5. The teacher asks students to make predictions about the remainder of the selection by asking questions like "What do you think the rest of the selection will be about?" and "Why do you think so?"

6. The teacher assigns the students to read the rest of the selection silently.

7. The teacher facilitates a follow-up discussion of the material.

Ms. Mueller, who wanted her students to become more critical thinkers, modified the existing ReQuest structure by asking different kinds of questions that involved more than just knowing about the information in the selections she chose for her students to read. Ms. Mueller decided to revisit the book *Building a New Land: African Americans in Colonial America* (Haskins & Benson, 2001) to scaffold this new way of asking questions. Ms. Mueller liked that the book was formatted into short accounts of two to four pages, which would be easy for her students to read and enjoy.

Ms. Mueller's ReQuest strategy is described below.

The students read silently. To begin their work with the ReQuest procedure of critical thinking, Ms. Mueller had her students read silently the first two paragraphs of "African Contributions to Colonial Society," a short piece in *Building a New Land.*

The students meet in CALCs. Students then got into their long-standing CALC groups and generated questions for the teacher.

The students question the teacher. When the students finished their question generation in their CALCs, they asked Ms. Mueller the following questions:

- Where were African traditions more developed than European ones?

- For what were the slaves respected?

- What was a popular pastime among White colonists?

- What African traditions influenced American ones in major ways?

- What is folklore?

- What do you think of divination?

- Is the occult always a bad thing?

The teacher answers students' questions, highlighting the types of questions asked. Answering their questions, Ms. Mueller also asked them to think about what kind of questions they asked. She pointed out that their questions focused on the literal comprehension level, which was good, "since I want my students to comprehend the information as well as become critical about it." By asking literal questions that could be answered directly from the text, Ms. Mueller knew that the students could comprehend the material, but they had not yet asked critical questions that would address issues of power, author intention, and language usage.

The teacher asks the students questions, highlighting the critical thinking involved. When she asked her questions, Ms. Mueller had her students think about the words *American, European, major, slaves,* and *respected.* She particularly had her students rethink the language in this second piece by demonstrating her own questions about the language used by the authors as well as the authors' tone toward the reader. She also highlighted how they had begun to think critically about language usage when they challenged the language usage from the short piece "Antonio, a Negro" in their last reading from the text (i.e., using *Black* and *African American* interchangeably).

The students critically discuss teacher-posed questions. Ms. Mueller pointed out to her students that when Holly worked with them, she had asked them why the authors used *African American* when the term was not in usage during colonial times, and especially when the reading from "Antonio" said that he was considered an "alien." Using this example, she asked the CALC to think about the five words she had highlighted—and the sentences they were in—while discussing the paragraph in which they were found.

The teacher initiates a follow-up discussion. Ms. Mueller brought to her students' awareness that language is powerful and can be harmful to some groups while privileging others. She also pointed out that sometimes language is used to show how people should be seen rather than the way we might stereotype them.

To help students learn about critical questioning of text and author bias, language practices that appear objective and authoritative, and perspectives given and others unseen, we created a list of questions that addressed these issues. Students could then become more critically aware that language and author stance are not objective and that they should learn to question the point of view taken. The questions, generated from "Antonio, a Negro," are as follows:

1. Why did slaves have to have permission to get married?

2. When did Antonio win his freedom?

3. Why did people need slaves to run their farms?

4. Why were Black folks called Negroes?

5. In what ways were the Bennetts good to Antonio? In what ways were they not?

6. How did John Casar get Black people to work for him, when he was also Black?

7. Why did the attitudes suddenly change against the Blacks?

8. Why did White people call them aliens if they weren't from another planet?

9. Why were there slave codes?

10. Why didn't White people treat Blacks the way they treated each other?

From the use of critical questioning in CALCs, we discovered that students learn the information from the text, but they also learn to see the way information can be biased toward or prejudiced against particular groups or ideas. We also found that critical questioning is easier in CALCs because students teach each other. The questions also involve students' connecting information to their own lives, other texts they have read, or their ideas of the world. By becoming familiar with questions that challenge the writing of the text, the author's perspective, and the language used in the text to discuss information, students learn that texts contain information that does the following:

• Allows for multiple interpretations

• Gives voice to the dominant worldview and often silences other perspectives

• Uses language in ways that can benefit some groups while being detrimental to other groups

Meeting the Needs of Struggling Students

From our experiences with question and problem posing in middle level classrooms, we have found that most students learn to pose questions within a short amount of time. There are others, however, who have more difficulty with question and problem posing. By working in a small group with students who have such difficulties, we know that teacher demonstrations are critical. Ms. Mueller works with her students in a small group while other content area literature circles are taking place around the room. She has also used two prompt sheets with these students as they learn to challenge the information they read. The first prompt sheet helps students with the basic information and consists of a modified "Five Ws":

- Who is presenting the information?
- What is the important message of the information?
- Why is the information presented this way?
- Where does this information fit with what you already know?
- When will this information be useful to you?

Her second prompt sheet asks questions of the students so they will eventually begin to ask similar questions themselves. By allowing her students to use these prompts while she models how to asks such questions, her students are better prepared to understand the information they read and to ask questions or pose problems about the information itself. The second prompt sheet lists the following questions:

- What do I know about this topic?
- What new information did I learn from the reading?
- What didn't I understand about the topic?
- What more could the author have told me about the topic?
- Why did the author write this piece?
- What would the author want me to know about the topic?
- What am I wondering about in relation to the topic?
- How would I tell someone else about this topic?
- How does my idea of the topic differ from the author's?
- Where do the author and I agree?
- What was the most interesting part of this passage?
- How could another person share this information?
- Is there another side of the story that could be shared?

Conclusion

Because students are always reading to learn and learning to read, they should be exposed to all types of information in their content classrooms. The use of different types of questions helps to produce stronger readers and language users. Coupled with this notion, however, is the reality that many types of questions flesh out learning across the curriculum. Question and problem posing works well for discussing informational texts and the efferent reading that is often part of content studies.

Question and problem posing gives students permission to connect new ideas to what they know, to discuss tangential information that fleshes out the topic they are studying, and to respond to others about their learning. Students enjoy asking questions of one another, and they can make predictions about the information they read. They connect to each other's ideas and take ownership of their knowledge acquisition in enjoyable and thought provoking ways. Although question and problem posing was a new way of thinking about content knowledge acquisition for the teachers we worked with, they quickly discovered that allowing students to generate their own questions helped their students to negotiate their own meanings and connections to science and social studies.

Chapter 8

Formative Assessment and Content Area Literature Circles

We know through our own experiences with a number of classrooms that not only do students benefit from content area literature circles (CALCs), their teachers do, too. The teachers we worked with discovered that the stories students tell in CALCs are an effective way of assessing the students' learning of content knowledge.

Teachers have access to a multitude of assessment tools to use with their students. Beginning where students are in their understanding of content knowledge and then selecting strategies to use is often a matter of deciding what a teacher wants to know about a student's learning and where the student is in terms of progress toward a negotiated goal. Because every student is unique in terms of personality, prior knowledge, history, and values, we need to keep each individual student in mind as we decide what they know and how they apply this knowledge. With such diversity within their CALCs, we can choose to assess students in four major ways:

- Self-assessment
- Peer assessment
- Teacher assessment
- A combination of the above

We think that a combination of these choices is the most powerful way to assess, and a way that gives voice to all members of the learning community. We also inform our students on which assessment or combination we will use for particular units or lessons so they can read, discuss, and study more purposefully.

Formative Assessment

Throughout any given unit of study, many teachers are continually assessing their students. When this assessment informs their teaching, it becomes the basis of their ongoing planning and directly impacts student learning. Rhodes and Shanklin (1993) assert that "effective assessment takes place most often in the midst of instruction and informs that instruction" (p. ix). As an ongoing part of instruction, formative assessment allows teachers to know what their students are learning and where they may need extra instruction (through mini-lessons or one-to-one sessions) to better understand either the content of the task at hand or the process by which the task must be completed.

Content area literature circles (CALCs), which allow for performance-based or authentic assessments, are much more powerful indicators of what students have learned than the quizzes and tests often used in middle-level classrooms. CALCs provide an authentic venue for students to engage in their content learning while also giving teachers the opportunity to hear and see what students do and do not know. Teachers can then create new opportunities for students to rethink, relearn, or revisit the content their students don't quite understand.

The teachers with whom we work have discovered that their students more often learn through social processes, and that their students' natural chattiness could lead to a pleasurable and purposeful accomplishment. This is an additional benefit of these assessment strategies. When Ms. Mueller was asked what she wanted her sixth-grade students to know from the unit on exploration, she replied, "I want them to know what distinguishes some exploratory endeavors from others. They should understand how some exploring nations worked within the native cultures and how others came and annihilated whole peoples." Once the students had finished with their questions for each other, Ms. Mueller reevaluated what they had learned and compared their learning to her purposes. She quickly asked students her own questions, which confirmed that the students did learn what she wanted.

The Purposes of Assessment

We assess content area literature circles (CALCs) for three major reasons:

- Recognizing what students have learned
- Meeting the diverse needs of our students
- Planning for future lessons

Once we have taught something to our students, we—along with many other stakeholders in the educational process—want to know that the students have actually learned what we wanted them to learn. Through informal assessments such as anecdotal records, journals, and student feedback, we can discover what our students know and what they still find challenging. In CALCs, students share what they are learning, and we are able to listen in on those discussions, which allows us to make decisions concerning our teaching, our students' understanding and misunderstanding, and the content materials they are using.

We also assess students to discover their particular needs and how we can facilitate those needs so that all children have the opportunity to learn the content we teach. By listening in on CALCs, reviewing students' self-assessments, and noting the questions they ask and don't ask, we can modify instruction to meet the needs of all our students. We can also make decisions about the materials we are using and the way we are using them.

Finally, we use formative assessments to help our own teaching. When we assess our students' knowledge, we are better able to plan future lessons. Sometimes we need to repeat a lesson or revise it to help our students grasp a particularly difficult concept. At other times we find that our students already know something we planned to teach, and we can gracefully abandon that for other content they might want to know or that we want to teach. We often find, through our use of formative assessments, that our students are learning far more than we thought they were.

Tools for Formative Assessment

There are numerous ways to assess students and a multitude of tools that will meet any teacher's needs or content-specific materials. We share the most useful formative assessment tools that we have used with our students, which allows both teachers and students a voice in classroom learning and in the ways in which we can all discover what it is we know and what we still need to consider in our content learning.

Audiotapes

Audiotaping is the most formal of the strategies for formative assessment. Audiotaping allows you to be everywhere at once, so to speak. When first initiating content area literature circles (CALCs), it can be useful to have students tape their discussions, both for you to hear and for them to hear. These can also be used as examples for you to use to discuss the positive ways for students to engage in a CALC. You can use audiotapes in two ways: The first is to simply listen to the tape and take notes. The other way is to transcribe the conversation and use the print copy to analyze your students' talk.

When audiotapes are used as an alternative to anecdotal records, we would recommend that they be used sporadically. From our own experience we know how difficult it would be to audiotape all CALCs in all of our classes. There are times, however, when we want to listen to our students as they talk about the books they are reading or the other materials they are using. By placing small recorders on tables when students were in their literature circles, we were able to listen later to the questions students generated in their discussions. Listening to particular groups as they created questions, teachers are then able to listen to the audiotapes of the other groups and discover where students have not quite "got it right," in terms of the information they are discussing or the questions they are asking. With this type of information, teachers can then plan mini-lessons about questioning skills or address misconceptions about content.

As you listen to the tape or read through a transcript, you should look for information in two general areas: content acquisition and CALC process. The CALC discussion on "Antonio, a Negro" from Chapter 1 will serve as our example here. From the transcription of that tape, Ms. Mueller determined that the students had a conceptual understanding of what prejudice is, the notion of *alien* in the context of racism, the idea of slavery and how it connects to citizenship historically, and an experiential understanding of racism and alienation (but not slavery). She also determined that the students were working well together as a CALC because they were able to clarify concepts for each other, made connections with each other's ideas, sparked one another's thinking, felt free to ask one another for clarification, and wondered about the implementation of the historical concepts they were discussing.

From this information, Ms. Mueller could decide whether to continue with her instruction as she had planned or teach concepts her students didn't understand. Whatever decision teachers make in terms of using audiotapes for assessment, the occasional use of them can be beneficial and really quite enlightening.

Student-Generated Assessments

Self-assessment allows students to reflect upon their own performances, content understandings, or presentation of what they are learning or know. This type of assessment also allows students to think about how they worked with others, what they learned through the content area literature circle (CALC), and how they think they performed on their presentation of knowledge. This is also a good place for students to communicate where they had comprehension breakdowns with the information they were studying, social breakdowns with others, or misunderstanding about CALCs and how discussion did or didn't work for them.

Three quick assessments used by the teachers we worked with included the following:

- *Exit cards.* These are used at the end of class and are sometimes called exit tickets. Students write what they have learned that day about content and/or process. This can also be done orally if time permits. When done orally, there can be no repetitions.

- *Written reflection with prompts.* This is a more involved written document, using open-ended prompts given by the teacher.

- *Spontaneous student-teacher interviews.* These are one-to-one interviews in which the teacher can confirm individual student knowledge. At the same time, students are encouraged to ask the teacher about concepts or content that they don't understand.

A more in-depth, student-generated assessment that the teachers used was the Self-Evaluation form (Appendix D). We have found that middle-level students are often hesitant to discuss their concerns or misunderstandings about content information or their roles in a group process. Thus, a self-evaluation form that addresses these concerns as well as the content under study can be enlightening for teachers. Students bring more than their prior knowledge about the content to any classroom; they bring their feelings of social adequacy or inadequacy and academic self-esteem as well. This self-evaluation form addresses both the social and the academic aspects of CALCs for middle-level learners.

Peer Conferences

Peer conferences take place after a series of content area literature circles (CALCs). The literature circle members meet in groups with the teacher to discuss the group's learning and process. The group brainstorms positive suggestions that could strengthen the process, and then reflects on what could be improved. From this brainstorming, each member of the group receives a multitude of choices about how to work with others and how to present the knowledge that he or she has learned. Eventually, the teacher will no longer meet with the group during their peer conferences, but they will report what they have discussed on a Peer Conference Feedback form (Appendix E) and a Personal Feedback form (Appendix F). Table 8-1 is an example of a Personal Feedback form that Vanessa filled out for the group once Ms. Mueller met with them and discussed their process and progress as a group.

Table 8-1.   Personal Feedback Form

Name: _Vanessa_   Date: _April 18_

Topic Under Discussion: _"Antonio, a Negro"_

Positive Feedback:
As a group we helped each other understand some of the things we didn't get and we also asked each other questions that made us think more about what we are reading. We liked working on the ideas together.

Problem With the Discussion:
The problems we had is that sometimes we don't listen to each other because we only want to talk ourselves. We also sometimes didn't come prepared to the group, so that took more time than if we did what we were supposed to do.

Ideas for Improvement:
We all agreed that we need to do our individual work first so that it doesn't waste time in the literature circle.

Peer conferences can also take place during a series of CALCs, and may include written feedback from each member to the teacher after reflecting on the process as he or she talks. For instance, Sally, a vociferous sixth grader in Ms. Mueller's class, found that she could not share her opinions with others because the group always wanted consensus. When she shared an alternative viewpoint, others saw that consensus could not be reached. Thus Sally learned to be silent in the content discussions during social studies. After observing the content discussions in which Sally did not talk, Ms. Mueller asked her to write up a Personal Feedback form about the process.

When Ms. Mueller read Sally's feedback about being silenced in the group due to the expectation of consensus, Ms. Mueller addressed this issue with the class. By addressing this with the whole class, Ms. Mueller found that this discussion freed a number of students from their self-imposed silences and allowed them to add more to the learning in the CALCs. Ms. Mueller also found that her first assessments of her students were misleading because the students had misunderstood the intent of the CALCs. Ms. Mueller realized that if she had not disrupted the process with her students, many would not have performed as she expected they would. Her ideas of who they were and what they knew would have been limited because the students were not engaging in the discussion, and thus they were in danger of disengaging from the learning process. By finding out why some of her students weren't talking, she was better able to evaluate her students' learning and address this problem with the whole class before everyone was formally assessed.

Anecdotal Records

Without the luxury of a lot of time, teachers can utilize Anecdotal Records (Appendix G) during content area literature circle (CALC) time. Many of the teachers we worked with were able to hear what their students were discussing in their small groups by walking around the room. Listening briefly to the conversations, the teachers were able to take anecdotal notes or just place check marks next to the names of students who were talking.

Briefly noting what kinds of questions the students asked about the information they were discussing was another way these teachers filled out their anecdotal records. They also checked the type of questions students were asking each other, which allowed the teachers to enter into the conversations at numerous "teachable moments" that addressed some of the topics the students were discussing. As young people discuss what they are learning in CALCs, teachers can monitor their use of specific vocabulary and conceptual ideas in a number of ways.

Wandering around the room, listening to our students as they discuss their learning, and then making brief notes about who said what allows us to be present with our students while also giving them space to talk without feeling judged. Some of our students shut down their talk when we come too close, and that is not our intention. By briefly jotting down what important points our students are making, we are able to validate their thinking in whole-class closure at the end of the period. Sometimes we use our notes to plan for teaching or to address the misconceptions students may have. Using a whole-class format to correct misconceptions doesn't put any student on the spot in terms of what he or she has shared in the small groups. Anecdotal notes can be filed for use the following year as well. We use them to see where students had the most difficulty with the concepts of a particular unit, so we can be sure to be more explicit the following year.

Content Area Question Matrix

The final way we assess student questioning in content area literature circles (CALCs) is through a Content Area Question Matrix (Appendix H), which lists types of questions students can ask as well as the types of information students can seek. A question matrix allows students and teachers a way to assess the types of questions students generate in CALCs. Table 8-2 is an example of a question matrix

Table 8-2. Content Area Question Matrix

Expository Text / Question Matrix	R Recall Question	C/E Cause & Effect	C/O Chronological Order	P/S Problem & Solution	D Description	I Inference	I/E Main Idea & Examples or Details	Expository Text / Question Matrix
Content	BP				AC	SV		Content
Concepts			AC				BP	Concepts
Issues	HI				AC	SV		Issues
Illustration	HI					HI		Illustration
Application								Application
Connection	SA		BP					Connection
Extension								Extension
Expository Text / Question Matrix	R Recall Question	C/E Cause & Effect	C/O Chronological Order	P/S Problem & Solution	D Description	I Inference	I/E Main Idea & Examples or Details	Expository Text / Question Matrix

that Ms. Mueller's students generated from their discussions on exploration. Students monitor the type of questions they ask by placing their initials inside the box that corresponds to the question they asked in their CALC.

By having students use the matrix while they are generating questions in their literature circles, teachers allow students to see what types of questions they ask. Often students ask very literal questions until they are aware of the limitations this type of questioning reaps in terms of information. By seeing the types of questions they can ask, students begin to flesh out their questioning repertoire and thus develop deeper understanding of the content under study. Teachers must first scaffold this information for students by explaining the different types of questions and the multiple ways of exploring a text. From our example, we could suggest that Ms. Mueller's students need to work more with cause and effect and with problem and solution types of questions. We cannot be sure, however, until we looked at the text the students read before their discussion. Some texts lend themselves more readily to cause and effect than others. Problem and solution, however, could be part of every text discussion if we wanted to highlight critical literacy skills. Then students could ask questions about the content of the text and the author's intentions, posing problems from either one and coming up with solutions to the problems they posed.

When we work with students on question and problem posing, we describe the types of questions we would like students to create while in their CALCs. We also explain the types of content that students can ask questions about, such as the written prose in a text, the figures, the captions, or the photographs. We often find that students don't use this additional information, which can be crucial to their understanding of the topic. We also discuss with students how some texts allow for different types of questions about specific types of information. Thus we do not push the idea that all types of questions should be asked, because some texts do not lend themselves to all questions.

After students generate questions in CALCs the first few times, we have the groups share those questions. That way, we can more fully discuss how some questions just don't fit the text being read. Another benefit of whole-class sharing is that students can see what types of questions are being asked, which guides them toward more diverse questions. A third benefit of this sharing is that teachers and students can see where certain students seem to have strengths in creating particular types of questions. Then, for future CALCs, students can be regrouped so that all students can learn from one another's strengths.

"Habits of Mind" Process

Assessing the idea of multiple perspectives is not an easy endeavor. We do find, however, that teachers can assess students' reasoning skills and whether or not students are beginning to think like critical consumers of knowledge. A way of asking students to think about their reasoning skills is through the "habits of mind" questions developed by the Central Park East School system in New York City. Focused on critical thinking, these five questions provide students with a structure for using reason and logic to support a position on an issue or problem. Table 8-3 lists the five questions, which invite students to think deeply and critically about what they have been reading and are currently discussing. The questions provide an organized format for forcing the discussants to support their opinions and ideas. The questions reinforce the notions of accuracy and authenticity as well as meaningfulness and importance. They also facilitate students' abilities to look at difficult issues and sort out truth from fiction and to cross content areas when the issues or problems are best handled through an integrated approach.

Table 8-3.   Habits of Mind

How do you know? The focus is on providing evidence. Here the students might go back into the readings to provide support for their views. They bring quotations, illustrations, facts, and figures to the group.

Who said it and why? The focus is on viewpoint. This asks the students to look carefully at the authenticity of the author. Who is he or she? What is his or her background? Does the author have the expertise to be writing on this topic in a definitive way?

What led to it? What else happened? The focus is on elements of cause and effect. Here students need to use reasoning to see that all the pieces fit together and make sense together. Could one detail be the cause of another? Does the information provide foreground or background for the issue or problem?

What if . . .? Suppose that . . .?" The focus is on hypothesizing. This too asks the students to go beyond the information itself to ascertain its connection with other ideas and issues within the same broad concept or topic. How does the knowledge and understanding gained here facilitate further knowledge gathering and understanding in new arenas?

Who cares? The focus is on relevance and importance. It is key that the students see the relevance of the information they are gathering. They need to understand how it fits both deeply and broadly so that they can move to the next facet with keen interest and appropriate background.

Meier (2002)

Journals and Learning Logs

By keeping journals or logs of the connections they make, students have an easier way of making further connections as they continue the study of a particular topic. When students record their connections, the following day's content area literature circle (CALC) is not so difficult to start in terms of students' remembering and accessing prior knowledge. Students also have a better idea of where to go next in their studies. Learning logs can take various forms, from Venn diagrams to poetry.

One we especially like to use with students is a modified Venn diagram, which allows students to think about how information does come together across content areas. Figure 8-1 is Shavaun's example, addressing the various topics and connections he found while thinking about and discussing *We Were There, Too!* (Hoose, 2001). Shavaun, an eighth grader working with Ms. Saunders on an inquiry about the role young people played in history, had perused the book and found that although everything and every person in it was linked by history, they also had ties to the other content areas. He thought that these biographies could be studied in the content areas he highlighted. We find Shavaun's example especially interesting because

Figure 8-1. Shavaun's Venn Diagram

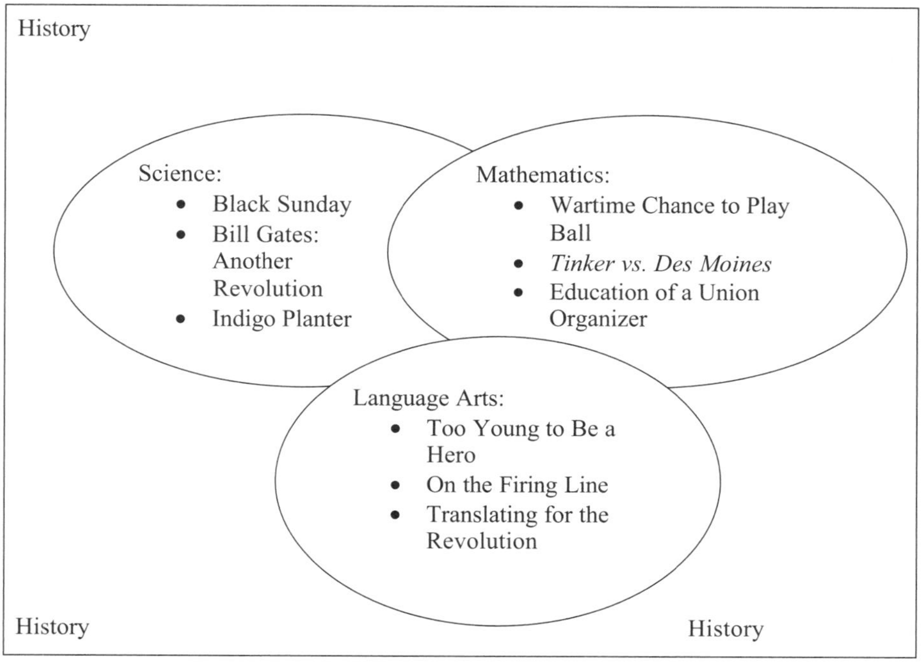

of the way he thought about how history is linked with other content areas. He started out thinking about young people's roles in history but found that young people were instrumental in geography, science, and mathematics as well. His Venn diagram lists the stories he found of interest and that connected to the other content areas.

PQP Forms

PQP forms (Appendix I) allow students to praise, question, and propose one another in a content area literature circle. In a typical PQP, group members are given praise for their ideas or contributions, become aware of where they weren't clear in presenting information, and are given suggestions for how to proceed in their next discussion. Group members, by looking for praiseworthy aspects of their peers' verbal interactions, become aware of the positive elements of presenting information to others while learning the information themselves.

By developing questions for each other, students become involved in understanding what information is being communicated and when they might be having comprehension breakdown. A proposed suggestion allows group members to become better informed about what might be missing in their own understandings of the topic under study or the best way to relate it to others.

Rubrics

A rubric can be used for content area literature circles (CALCs) to help students understand teacher expectations. We don't suggest that rubrics be used often, because students come to view them as the "only and correct" way of talking about and knowing content information. Yet when learning about CALCs students do appreciate knowing the multiple ways they can think about the content under study.

After learning the basic elements about transforming what they read in texts into verbal information for other students' understandings, scrutiny, or enjoyment, students no longer need a rubric. Rather, we ask students to use their individual creativity to engage the information and each other in CALCs.

We often generate a rubric with students that addresses classroom expectations for learning. Appendix J is an example of a checklist rubric that reminds students of what may be important to discuss in a CALC.

Conclusion

The formative assessment strategies described in this chapter can be used across the curriculum and throughout content studies. Through such assessments, your students will have an opportunity to display the understanding they have gained and how they connect that knowledge to their own experiences and lives. Giving students the opportunity to present their knowledge of science, math, and social studies knowledge through the stories they tell about themselves in connection to the content they are learning will build student confidence, help them with organizing information, allow them to problem-pose or problem-solve, and create opportunities for critical thinking and reasoning. It will also give them a sense of ownership and independence.

Chapter 9

Content Area Literature Circles in the Curriculum

Content area literature circles (CALCs) are an exciting way for students to learn content knowledge. As we have explained, numerous benefits make CALCs a viable way for engaging students in any of their content subjects. By carefully planning for CALCs, content teachers can produce learning environments which students are actively participating in their own learning. Planning for CALCs for the first time can seem overwhelming, however, especially when discussion has not been a primary means of learning for the students.

In this chapter, we present the ways we have planned for CALCs during one day, in one thematic unit, and across the academic year. We accomplish this by working with Ms. Mueller, the sixth-grade teacher in Texas who teaches language arts through units based on social studies content.

Fitting Content Area Literature Circles Into the Curriculum

Deciding how to use content area literature circles (CALCs) in the classroom is perhaps an easy first step. Determining how to use them in the curriculum may be more difficult. When Ms. Mueller first started using CALCs in her classrooms, she moved slowly, trying them first with one lesson plan, then with one unit, and eventually working them into her yearly curriculum plans.

Planning for CALCs Within the Day

Using content area literature circles (CALCs) starts with a daily lesson plan. In the following example, we show how Ms. Mueller planned to use CALCs to help her students understand the concept of social justice in their social studies class. Ms. Mueller teaches two groups of students who have various abilities and learning styles. She teaches one group language arts, reading, and social studies during a block in the morning, and the other group in the afternoon. Students often move in and out of her classroom for music, computer, library, and specialized reading or tutoring classes throughout the day.

In Ms. Mueller's class, this lesson can be completed in one day. For teachers who are restricted to single periods of 48–55 minutes, this lesson plan would take 2–3 days to complete. The first day would be used for setting up the lesson, allowing students to complete the reading and to prepare for CALCs the next day. On the second day, students participate in CALCs and then begin to create graphic organizers to present to the rest of the class or to hang in the hallway to share with others in their building. On the third day, students finish and post their graphic organizers.

Table 9-1 shows one of 15 lesson plans that Ms. Mueller has created for a unit that addresses issues of social justice. During the first week of the unit, Ms. Mueller used picture books to help her students begin to understand social justice. This lesson plan is used in the second week. Ms. Mueller uses CALCs twice a week during this unit, relying on them as a lesson in "initiating a discussion." She uses CALCs more extensively in units that require her students to read longer texts than the ones used in this unit, which concentrates more on picture books because the concept of social justice is a difficult one for many of her sixth graders.

In this lesson plan, Ms. Mueller explains the goal of her lesson, the materials she will need, the basic outline of how the lesson should proceed, and how she will assess what her students have learned. The plan appears rather formal because this is the way Ms. Mueller writes her lesson plans for other teachers' use. Ms. Mueller uses the Thinking during Reading form (Appendix B), graphic organizers (discussed in chapter 4), and the Self-Evaluation forms (Appendix D).

Table 9-1. Social Justice Lesson Plan

Goal: One way to have students think about the issue of social justice is to introduce it through literature that is written for them. Through discussions of literature that address working conditions of children around the world, middle school students can begin to understand that life is not equal, equitable, or fair for many young people.

Objectives (students will be able to):

1. List what they have learned from the reading selection
2. Explain the working conditions that would be difficult for them
3. Isolate the key ideas found in the reading selection
4. Determine why children must work in some parts of the world
5. Describe three types of child labor that exist in the world today
6. List where child labor exists in the world

Assessment: Students are assessed through the Thinking During Reading form, participation in content area literature circles, graphic organizers, and the Self-Assessment form.

Materials:

1. Copies of *Listen to Us: The World's Working Children* (Jane Springer, 1997)
2. Thinking During Reading form—one for each student
3. Butcher paper and crayons, colored pencils, or markers—one set for each CALC
4. Pencils or pens for writing on the Thinking During Reading form
5. Overhead transparency—prompts for initiating discussion (used only if students are unfamiliar with CALCs), including:
   - What was the most interesting part of the reading?
   - What did you think about the reading?
   - What was the most important part of the reading?
   - What facts did you learn?
   - How is this like your life?
   - What would your life be like if you had to work as these young people did?
6. Self-Evaluation form

Lesson Outline:	Time:
Day 1	

1. Begin lesson by asking students about "work."
  a. Who works in your family?
  b. What kind of work do you do?
  c. Why should young people work?
  d. Why shouldn't they work?
  e. When does work become unfair to young people?
	10 minutes

2. Introduce the reading through a short book talk.	3 minutes
3. Divide students into five groups by counting them off.	2 minutes

4. Give assignments to students by their number.
  a. All No. 1s read: "What Is Child Labor?" (pp. 10–16)
  b. All No. 2s read: "Why Do Children Work?" (pp. 17–23)
  c. All No. 3s read: "Where Do We Find Child Labor?" (pp. 25–29)
  d. All No. 4s read: "What Work Do Children Do?" (pp. 30–37)
  e. All No. 5s read: "What Work Do Children Do?" (pp. 58–66)
	3 minutes

5. Students read selections and fill in the Thinking During Reading form.	30 minutes

(continued)

Table 9-1.   Social Justice Lesson Plan (*Continued*)

Day 2	
1. Begin the day by moving students into CALCs.	4 minutes
a. Create the membership of each group *before* students arrive. Each group has five members—one of each number.	
b. Post a list of each group on the blackboard for students to see as they enter the room.	
2. Place prompts on the overhead and remind students to also use their Thinking During Reading form to begin their CALCs.	1 minute
3. Monitor the CALCs by walking around the room.	20 minutes
4. Transition students to working on graphic organizers by asking the entire class to brainstorm graphic organizers they could use to present their information. (Types of organizers are posted on walls.)	7 minutes
5. Students select appropriate graphic organizer for their group's purpose and begin work.	15 minutes
Day 3	
1. Students continue in groups working on graphic organizers.	30 minutes
2. Groups share their organizers with class or post in hallway.	10 minutes
3. Students assess their participation on Self-Evaluation forms.	7 minutes

Planning for CALCS During the Month

Ms. Mueller teaches social studies in units. She often uses the textbook adopted by her school district, but at other times she uses available literature, movies, and Internet resources to help her sixth-grade students acquire the knowledge expected of them in Texas.

One of her units is on the continent of Africa. Ms. Mueller's students often ask her about places they know about but have seldom studied in their first five years of school. In the last two years of her teaching, she has come to believe that her students' interests in places other than the Western world should be addressed.

Appendix K is a unit plan that Ms. Mueller uses to teach her students about the regions of Africa and their geography, history, and cultures. In this plan, Ms. Mueller includes a list of the materials she will use to teach her students, but she does not make it as detailed as her daily lesson plans. She plans by the week rather than the day, and she also consults the textbook to frame her unit. This unit takes five weeks to complete and involves a research project and presentation that are the focus of the unit's last two weeks. Ms. Mueller often plans this unit for near the end of the school year, when she is attempting to balance students' interests with their desires to be finished with school completely. Because Ms. Mueller integrates language arts, reading, and social studies, she uses both informational texts and novels in her teaching. (Table 9-2 lists the materials used for this unit.) Her students are also familiar with content area literature circles (CALCs), the strategies Ms. Mueller has highlighted throughout the year, word walls (chapter 5), and research procedures. Although this unit emphasizes how often CALCs can be used as well as their different purposes, Ms. Mueller does use CALCs less often in other units. This unit on Africa, and Ms. Mueller's use of inquiry as the primary means of learning, makes the use of CALCs more feasible.

Table 9-2. List of Materials in Regions of Africa Unit

Novels
A Girl Named Disaster (Farmer, 1998)
Somehow Tenderness Survives: Stories of Southern Africa (Rochman, 1988)
Zulu Dog (Ferreira, 2002)
No Condition Is Permanent (Kessler, 2000)
Beyond the Mango Tree (Zemser, 2000)
The Storyteller's Beads (Kurtz, 1998)
The Baboon King (Quintana, 1999)
Yakabou Must Choose (Perry, 2001)

Picture Books
Day of Ahmed's Secret (Parry, 1995)
Galimoto (Williams, 1991)
Kofi and His Magic (Angelou, 2003)
Beatrice's Goat (McBrier, 2001)
The Village That Vanished (Grifalconi, 2002)
Fly, Eagle, Fly: An African Fable (Gregorowski, 2000)
My Rows and Piles of Coins (Lewis, 1999)
The Orphan Boy (Morin, 1995)
Fatuma's New Cloth (Bulion, 2002)
My Great-Grandmother's Gourd (Kessler, 2002)
The Storytellers (Lewin, 1998)
Gugu's House (Stock, 2001)
If You Should Hear a Honey Guide (Schindler, 2000)
The Village of Round and Square Houses (Grifalconi, 1986)
Sense Pass King: A Story from Cameroon (Tchana, 2002)

Informational Texts
A Is for Africa (Onyefulu, 1997)
Africa Is Not a Country (Knight et al., 2002)
Cat Mummies (Trumble, 1999)
The Maasai of East Africa: Celebrating the Peoples and Civilizations of Africa (Hetfield & Johnston, 2003)

(continued)

Table 9-2.   **List of Materials in Regions of Africa Unit** *(Continued)*

Informational Texts *(Continued)*

Egypt: The People (Moscovitch, 2000)

Peoples of the Desert (Low, 2003)

Nigeria: The Culture (Rosenberg & Kalman, 2003)

San (Heritage Library of African Peoples, South Africa) (Biesele, Elusbe, & Royal, 1997)

South Africa: The Culture (Clark, 2000)

Traditions From Africa (Golding, 1998)

An Egyptian Pyramid (Morley & Bergin, 2001)

The African Slave Trade (Newman, 2000)

African Beginnings (Haskins, 1998)

Morocco (Countries Faces and Places) (Merrick, 2000)

Exploration Into Africa (Ibazebo, 2000)

The Yoruba of West Africa (Hetfield, 2000)

Zimbabwe: Enchantment of the World Series (Rogers & Rogers, 2002)

Sahara: The Biggest Desert (Weintraub, 2003)

The End of Apartheid: A New South Africa (Tames, 2001)

Africa: A Cultural Atlas for Young People (Murray & Sheehan, 2003)

The Nile: Great Rivers of the World (Cumming, 2003)

Inside the Dzanga Sangha Rain Forest: Exploring the Heart of Central Africa (Lyman, 2001)

Africa (Continents) (Regan & Cremin, 1997)

Great Zimbabwe (Bessire, 1999)

Shaka: King of Zulus (Stanley, 1994)

Cleopatra: Goddess of Egypt, Enemy of Rome (Brooks, 1995)

Hatshepsut: His Majesty, Herself (Andronik, 2001)

Kings and Queens of West Africa (Diouf, 2000)

Ancient Africa: Modern Rhymes for Ancient Times (Altman, Lechman, & Perrone, 2002)

Movies

Born Free (1962)

Tarzan (1996)

Africa—The Serengeti (1994)

Portrait of Africa (Tapestry Series) (1989)

Travel by Train: Africa (1999)

Web sites

www.allAfrica.com

www.africanaperture.com

www.pbs.org/wnet/africa

www.lib.utexas.edu/maps/africa

www.afrika.no

www.h-net.org/gateways/africa

www.africam.com

Looking closely through Appendix L, you will see how often Ms. Mueller uses CALCs for much of her students' learning. She uses CALCs for vocabulary development, reading and responding to the content under study, support for each CALC member's research and learning, analysis of content, and evaluation purposes. Most of the CALCs are first and second stage (see chapter 1); the third stage is used only after the completion of an assignment.

Planning for CALCs Across the Year

Ms. Mueller plans and teaches language arts, reading, and social studies through a variety of units that extend across the academic year. In planning these units, Ms. Mueller also thinks about when would be the best time to introduce her students to particular processes of learning, such as applying research techniques, using graphic representations, thinking like a historian, and participating in content area literature circles (CALCs). She prepared a global curricular plan to address specific content and learning processes (Table 9-3).

Table 9-3. Global Plan for Social Studies

August
Introductions and Assessment
  a. Introduce learning logs.
  b. Introduce textbook.
  c. Have students read trade books.
  d. Introduce "thinking like historians, geographers, and anthropologists."
  e. Students write short personal narratives.
  f. Introduce student read-alouds for reading comprehension.
	October
	Unit Two: Social Justice (5-week unit)
	  a. Introduce KFN for vocabulary
	  b. CALCs—2nd & 3rd phases
	  c. Introduce rubric for CALCs
	  d. Introduce self-evaluation
	  e. Introduce Internet search techniques
	  f. Introduce ReQuest strategy
	  g. Short story or personal narrative
	  h. Computer research project as presentation

September
Unit One: Understanding Geography—Physical, Human, and Cultural (4-week unit)
  a. Introduce graphic organizers
  b. Introduce CALCs—1st phase
  c. Introduce word wall for vocabulary
  d. Introduce reader response through "say something" strategy
  e. Learning logs
  f. Graphic organizer as presentation
	November
	Unit Three: North America—History, Geography, & Culture (6-week unit)
	  a. Introduce pyramid organizer
	  b. Introduce "questioning the author"
	  c. Introduce think-alouds in CALCs and silent reading for comprehension
	  d. Introduce cubing for vocabulary

(continued)

Table 9-3.   Global Plan for Social Studies (Continued)

<table>
<tr><td valign="top">

December
Finish Unit Three:
  a. Introduce QAR strategy
  b. Introduce concept mapping and semantic webs
  c. Introduce "meeting of the minds"
  d. Use vocabulary matrix in CALCs
  e. Use Wondering As We Read form for CALC preparation
  f. Drama as presentation

January
Unit Four: Europe & Russia (3-week unit)
  a. Word wall & pyramid
  b. CALCs for reading comprehension (all levels)
  c. ReQuest strategy in CALCs
  d. Graphic organizer for presentation

Unit Five: Asia (3-week unit)
  a. "Say something" in CALC read-alouds
  b. QAR in CALCs
  c. Essay as presentation
  d. Word wall
  e. Learning logs
  f. Biography as presentation

February
Unit Five (Asia continued)

Unit Six: Oceana (2-week unit)
  a. Film: *Travel the World by Train: Australia and New Zealand* (1999)
  b. Internet research
  c. CALC support for research
  d. Picture-book creation as presentation

</td><td valign="top">

March
Unit Six: Latin America (2-week unit)
  a. "Questioning the author" & trade books on Latin American countries (politics & culture)
  b. Think-alouds in CALCs
  c. Cubing for vocabulary
  d. Concept map for presentation

Unit Seven: Mexico & Central America (3-week unit)
  a. "Meeting of the minds" in CALCs
  b. "Save the last word for me" in CALCs
  c. QAR strategy review
  d. Pyramid organizer
  e. Self-evaluations
  f. Drama as presentation

April
Tests and test preparation

May
Unit Eight: Africa (5-week unit)
  a. CALCs (all levels)
  b. Various graphic organizers
  c. Word walls & KFN for vocabulary
  d. "Save the last word for me"
  e. "Say something"
  f. ReQuest strategy
  g. Movie: *Portrait of Africa*
  h. Self-evaluations
  i. Inquiry projects for presentation

June
Finish Africa Unit

</td></tr>
</table>

When preparing her global schedule, Ms. Mueller began by addressing the following questions:

- What do I want my students to know and/or do when they leave my class?

- What content knowledge is especially significant for my students to learn?

- What literacy processes do I want my students to learn?
- What are the best possible ways to engage my students in learning?
- What strategies and skills will benefit my students in the future?

Other issues Ms. Mueller addresses at the beginning of the year include questions about assessment. Thus, during the first 2 weeks of school she is intent upon knowing her students and their learning skills. She has expressed that "I need to know what my students already know in terms of content knowledge, world experiences, and learning strategies. But I also need to find out about their language arts skills as well—their reading, writing, responding, listening, and discussion skills. Once I assess those, we are ready."

Ms. Mueller knows, however, that her global plan must change to fit the needs of her students. It focuses on introducing a number of strategies over the first semester and "really working on them during particular units so students will put them in their strategy toolboxes." She then spends the next semester asking her students to utilize those skills by reviewing those strategies in subsequent units. There have been years, however, when Ms. Mueller has had to continue to introduce strategies during the second semester because her students' learning skills were not where she wanted them to be. To help her students "catch up," she would spend more time on each strategy, thus pushing some back to be learned during the second half of the year.

Conclusion

Whether you decide to use content area literature circles (CALCs) one day or unit at a time, or to use them as a consistent part of your teaching across the year, the benefits for both you and your students are well worth your planning efforts. Through the use of strategies like CALCs that engage students in their learning, you utilize students' natural social instincts in the learning process. Because students' talk is observable, you are better able to assess what they know and what you need to plan for the next day, the next unit, or the next year.

Appendixes

Appendix A

Content Literature Review Sheet

Bibliographic Information: Author, date, title, city, publisher

Content/Concepts Addressed:

Summary (one paragraph):

Text Structure:

Evidence of Authenticity:

Evidence of Accuracy:

New Vocabulary or terminology:

Response to the Text:

Concept Load:
Hard
Just Right
Easy

Text Support:
Graphics:
Glossary:
Index:
Appendixes:
References:

Response to Visuals and Illustrations:

Appendix B

Thinking During Reading Form

Part I

Name:_____   Date:_____

Passage Read:_____

Author:_____ Number of Pages:_____

General Impressions:

Misunderstandings:

Connections to My Life, Another Subject, or the World:

Information That's Missing:

Predictions Made During Reading:

Thinking During Reading Form *(Continued)*

Part II

Name:_____ Date:_____

Title of Book:

Reason for Reading This Book:

_____

Three Ideas to Share in CALC:

1.

2.

3.

_____

After CALC

New Ideas From Others:

How Discussion Helped Me Understand:

Thinking During Reading Form *(Continued)*

Further Use

How This Information Will Help With My Project:

Appendix C

Wondering As We Read Form

Wondering As We Read Form

Name: _____ Date: _____

Topic:

What I wanted to know:

    a.

    b.

    c.

What I wondered while I was reading:

    a.

    b.

What I want to wonder about with my CALC group:

    a.

    b.

What our CALC still wants to know (after discussion):

Appendix D

Self-Evaluation Form

Name:_____   Date:_____

    Title of Inquiry Project:_____

I enjoyed engaging in CALC: 1   2   3   4   5   6   7   8   9   10
                             Not at all   Somewhat   A great deal

My effort in the discussion: 1   2   3   4   5   6   7   8   9   10
                         Not as good   About normal   Better than usual

I most enjoyed discussing:

The best thing about discussing the information:

What I enjoyed least about discussing the information:

Some things I learned about this topic:

Some things I learned about presenting what I knew:

What might have worked better in the discussion:

Who especially helped me to understand the information:

What created hurdles for me in this discussion:

Adapted from L. Bridges (1995)

Appendix E

Peer Conference Feedback Form

Group Members Present: Date:_____

Positive Elements of CALC Discussions:
Where Our Group Needs Improvement:
Ideas We Brainstormed for Improving Discussion:
How We Can Improve Our Understanding of Content:

Appendix F

Personal Feedback Form

Name: _____   Date:_____

Topic Under Discussion:_____

Positive Feedback:

Problem With the Discussion:

Ideas for Improvement:

Directions: Use this form to discuss information that you would like the teacher to consider when deciding about content area literature circles in the future. What worked well for you? What do you wish could have happened? What ideas do you want to share with the teacher? This is a personal form, so it should not be shared with others. This information is for the teacher only.

Appendix G

Anecdotal Record Form

Anecdotal Record/Check List		

Notes for Reteaching:

Appendix H

Content Area Question Matrix

Expository Text Question Matrix	R Recall Question	C/E Cause & Effect	C/O Chronological Order	P/S Problem & Solution	D Description	I Inference	I/E Main Idea & Examples or Details	Expository Text Question Matrix
Content								Content
Concepts								Concepts
Issues								Issues
Illustration								Illustration
Application								Application
Connection								Connection
Extension								Extension

This matrix is a modification of the "Think Trix Matrix" by Frank Lyman (1987).

Appendix I

PQP Form

Topic Under Discussion:_____

Group Member:_____   Date:_____

Praise: What I found especially good about what you said

Question: What I didn't quite understand about what you said

Propose: Something you might want to think about next time we meet in a circle

Reviewer:_____

Directions: Fill this out for one of your group members (your teacher will assign you a person or you can decide as a discussion group who will write up a PQP for whom). Give constructive feedback so all members of your content area literature circle can learn as you continue to discuss topics throughout the year.

Appendix J

Rubric for Content Area Literature Circle

Name:_____ Date:_____

Topic Discussed:_____

Discussion of Content Information
- Is clear and organized
- Contains examples and definitions for specific concepts and vocabulary
- Explains why this information is important to understanding the topic
- Connects to group's prior knowledge
- Contains bridging analogies for one another's understanding

Visual or Interactive Strategies
- Are clear and enhance information shared verbally
- Are large enough so each member can see them
- Invite other group members to question, share, or revisit

Presentation Manner
- Spoken to whole group so all could hear
- Spoken at a pace that is responsive to group's needs
- Organized, so pace is engaging for discussion
- Passion or interest displayed in the material being discussed or shared
- Time left for other group members' feedback

Listening Behavior
- Appropriate for each member to hear and share
- Each member shares at least once in the discussion
- Each member responds in ways that build confidence in other students' sharing

After reading the above criteria and remembering how the discussion with your group went, write a short evaluation of yourself as a member of your content area literature circle:

Appendix K

Africa: Its Geography, History, and Cultures

Goal: Addressing how the geography, history, and cultures of one continent influence one another is a way for sixth graders to realize that the diversity of a continent is the result of many factors. Because middle school students don't often study Africa, they miss an essential connection to American history.

Objectives (students will be able to):

1. Describe the various land regions of Africa and their characteristics
2. Explain how physical geography influences the culture and history of a place
3. Interpret and create physical and political maps of the regions of Africa
4. Use and interpret charts for resource purposes
5. List reasons for historical phenomena
6. Categorize information based on cultural, historical, or geographical factors
7. Determine the similarities and differences between their own geography and that of one African region
8. Analyze one culture of Africa and its influence on the world (research project)
9. Discuss and justify their ideas in small-group settings
10. Present their current learning to their classmates and school community

Materials:

1. Copies of textbook (Ms. Mueller uses *World Explorer*)

2. Learning logs for each student

3. Internet capability and time in the computer lab

4. Graph paper for maps

5. Colored pencils, markers, or crayons and butcher paper

6. Multiple copies of five novels, five picture books, and five informational texts

7. Transparencies of Re-Quest, KFN, "say something," and "save the last word for me" strategies, Personal Feedback forms, Rubric for Content Area Literature Circle, Self-Evaluation forms, Wondering As We Read forms, and various graphic organizers

8. Blank transparencies for overhead projector

Unit Outline:	*Time*
Week One: Introduction and Geography of a Continent	
Monday:	
1. Introduction to unit: students free-write what they know about Africa, especially its history, cultures, and geography. Teacher asks students to find Africa on the world map or globe.	15 minutes
2. Students work on political map of Africa, using Internet, textbooks, and *From Afar to Zulu*. Students work in pairs and write 12 facts or questions about geography of Africa for class discussion.	45 minutes
3. Students present questions and facts to class. Whole-class discussion on geography of Africa. Lists on butcher paper. Teacher presents major regions of Africa.	25 minutes
4. Students work in small groups (two pairs form one group of four) to find characteristics of one major region of Africa (South, Central, West, East, North).	20 minutes
5. Students begin a graphic organizer of their information.	15 minutes
6. Teacher transitions to book talks about the five novels students may read as part of this unit. Students list top three choices.	15 minutes
Tuesday:	
1. Read-aloud from *The Village That Vanished*.	15 minutes
2. Students discuss text in CALCs and brainstorm issues for whole-class discussion.	25 minutes
3. Whole-class discussion of issues from *The Village That Vanished*. Teacher writes major issues on butcher paper.	25 minutes
4. Teacher transitions to lecture on characteristics of region and geography of *The Village That Vanished*.	25 minutes
5. Students finish graphic organizers from Monday.	30 minutes
6. Students present and post graphic organizers.	15 minutes
Wednesday:	
1. Teacher hands out novels to small groups. (These groups will meet as CALCs for rest of unit.)	10 minutes
2. Students meet in small groups to negotiate reading of novel. (Students decide how far to read, and how long the novel will take to complete.)	15 minutes

3. Students begin novels.	25 minutes
4. Teacher transitions to class discussion on novels and their geographical location and reminds students of "setting."	20 minutes
5. Teacher assigns physical maps of Africa to work on in CALCs.	20 minutes
6. Students meet in CALCs to fill in maps.	10 minutes
7. Teacher assigns short reading from textbook, "Humans and Physical Geography" (4 pages), and asks students to list vocabulary or concepts new to them in their learning logs (e.g., Tropic of Capricorn, Tropic of Cancer).	30 minutes
8. Students read novels for homework and respond to novel.	
Thursday:	
1. Teacher checks progress of textbook assignment from Wednesday. Students finish reading.	10 minutes
2. Teacher assigns students to vocabulary discussion in CALCs and posts KFN strategy on overhead. Students meet in CALCs and create a word list using KFN, while teacher creates "Words Connected to Africa" for word wall.	15 minutes 25 minutes
3. Whole class lists new vocabulary words, and teacher writes them on word wall.	30 minutes
4. Teacher assigns students to read novels silently and to add vocabulary words to their learning logs.	30 minutes
5. Teacher transitions students to whole-class discussion about new vocabulary from novels to add to word wall. Teacher suggests that words can be categorized (e.g., geography words, culture words).	30 minutes
6. Students read novels for homework and list questions they have about the geography of the book's setting.	
Friday:	
1. Students read novels and look for quote for "save the last word for me" strategy. Teacher posts strategy on overhead.	25 minutes
2. Students meet in CALCs and complete "save the last word for me."	30 minutes
3. Class meets as a whole group and discusses the novels they are reading, the geography involved, and the issues in the texts. Teacher writes issues on overhead transparency. Student helper writes geography on chalkboard.	35 minutes

4. Teacher asks students to meet in CALCs and discuss one issue from list generated that is geography related. Students are asked to look for evidence of this issue in their novel.	25 minutes
5. Student groups share their issue and its evidence. Teacher wraps up geography topic with question for students to address in their learning logs: How is geography connected to the problems people face, the way they live, the things they value?	20 minutes
6. Students read their novels over the weekend.	
Week Two: The Cultures of Africa	
Monday:	
1. Teacher reads aloud from *Fatuma's New Cloth*, then asks the students to think about the setting, how it is different from what they know, and what activities are different. Teacher addresses the definition of *culture* and relates it back to *Fatuma's New Cloth*.	35 minutes
2. Students work in CALCs to figure out the aspects of culture in picture books: *Galimoto, Beatrice's Goat, The Village of Round and Square Houses, Gugu's House, The Orphan Boy*	35 minutes
3. Teacher posts semantic web organizer on overhead, and students create semantic webs of information they gathered.	35 minutes
4. Students share their ideas as whole class.	20 minutes
5. Students read novels with purpose of finding out about the culture in the text. Write ideas on Thinking During Reading forms or in learning logs.	15 minutes
6. Students read novels for homework and list questions about culture.	
Tuesday:	
1. Students meet in CALCs to discuss *culture* and list issues and ideas from novel about culture.	20 minutes
2. Students share issues with entire class, and teacher writes issues and ideas on overhead transparency. Students and teacher categorize issues and ideas (i.e., living in a desert region, drought conditions, fishing rights in coastal waters, issues of gender and privilege)	20 minutes
3. Students regroup in CALCs and discuss one category of issues or ideas that is applicable to their novel. Students find evidence in their books.	20 minutes
4. Whole-class discussion on how geography influences culture.	30 minutes

5.	Teacher assigns textbook chapter "Africa: Rich in Culture."	25 minutes
	a. Students select the region they might be interested in researching or the one that is highlighted in their novel. (Regions of Africa in textbook are: North, West, South, East.)	
	b. Students write in their learning logs four facts that they learn about the culture of one region.	
6.	Whole-class discussion of information from textbooks.	20 minutes
7.	Students read novels so as to be finished by the following Monday.	
Wednesday:		
1.	Working in CALCs, students create an inquiry chart to begin their thinking for their research projects, using information from the textbook.	30 minutes
2.	Whole-class meeting to discuss each group's findings and questions for inquiry or research projects.	30 minutes
3.	Students read textbook sections on their specific regions to gather more information and questions about their regions.	30 minutes
4.	Teacher reads aloud from *A Is for Africa* and invites students to "say something" to make connections about their region.	30 minutes
5.	Students work in CALCs to continue talking about their region and its cultural highlights, then make a list of cultural issues and ideas.	15 minutes
6.	Students read novels for homework.	
Thursday:		
1.	Teacher leads whole-class discussion about stereotypes, Africa, and the differences in regions. Students respond in learning logs.	25 minutes
2.	Students meet in CALCs to determine whether the list of cultural ideas contains stereotypes or actualities, then they make a chart to show realities vs. stereotypes.	30 minutes
3.	Students read novels and think about cultural stereotypes. Respond in learning logs.	30 minutes
4.	Students meet in CALCs to discuss the issue of stereotyping in their novels.	25 minutes
5.	Teacher wraps up class with discussion of particular stereotypes and the harm they cause individuals, groups of people, whole cultures, and continents.	25 minutes

Friday:	
1. Students work in CALCs to present information on culture from their novels and textbook regions.	50 minutes
a. Students determine what to share and how to share it.	
b. Students create a visual to represent their learning.	
2. Students present information to class and post it in hallway.	30 minutes
3. Teacher leads whole-class discussion on what questions students have about their region, its geography, and its culture.	45 minutes
a. Teacher writes questions on butcher paper or transparency.	
b. Students write questions of particular interest in their learning logs.	
c. Students theorize answers to their own and others' questions.	
4. Teacher reads aloud from *Africa Is Not a Country*.	10 minutes
5. Students finish reading novels over weekend.	
Week Three: History of Africa	
Monday:	
1. Students meet in CALCs to discuss novels.	35 minutes
a. Discuss initial thoughts about entire novel.	
b. Brainstorm issues to discuss at next CALC.	
c. Write about one issue in learning log.	
2. Teacher transitions to whole group lesson on ReQuest strategy.	45 minutes
a. Guided practice of strategy with textbook reading, "Africa: Shaped by History" (section 1, "Africa's First People").	
b. Discuss strategy process and students' response.	
3. Teacher assigns textbook reading, "Africa: Shaped by History," sections 2 and 3.	25 minutes
4. Students meet in CALCs for independent practice of ReQuest.	25 minutes
5. Students fill in Personal Feedback forms.	15 minutes
Tuesday:	
1. Students meet in CALCs to discuss issues in novel.	30 minutes
a. Find evidence in novel.	
b. Determine further issues for next discussion or discussion of group process.	

2. Teacher leads whole-class discussion on presentation of information and issues in novel and writes ideas on transparency.	30 minutes
3. Teacher transitions to historical connection of novel, and the history of Africa discussed in textbooks.	45 minutes
a. Reviews comparison and contrast skill.	
b. Addresses historical connection to stereotypes.	
4. Students meet in CALCs to discuss history of novel and connection of history and stereotypes, then list ideas.	15 minutes
5. Teacher wraps up with questions about Africa today. What do we know? What do we want to know? Students write in logs.	5 minutes
Wednesday:	
1. Teacher asks students about what they know and what they want to know, then makes connections to history of Africa.	25 minutes
2. Teacher assigns students to review textbook sections on their African regions, looking for historical connections to what is occurring presently. Students write ideas in learning logs.	20 minutes
3. Students meet in CALCs to discuss connections and theorize about historical phenomena.	25 minutes
4. Whole class meets and students share what they discussed in CALCs.	25 minutes
5. Teacher transitions to chart on issues and ideas about geography and culture, and invites students to add information that is connected to history.	40 minutes
6. Teacher wraps up with prompt about vocabulary from history section. What words are known, familiar, or new? Prepare for tomorrow.	5 minutes
Thursday:	
1. Teacher initiates vocabulary discussion and places new words on word wall.	25 minutes
2. Students meet in CALCs and discuss process of discussions over novel, then fill in Self-Evaluation forms.	45 minutes
3. Teacher transitions to whole class lesson on discussing informational texts in CALCs. Places Rubric for Content Area Literature Circle on overhead.	45 minutes
a. Reads aloud from *Cat Mummies*.	
b. Whole-class discussion with attention to rubric.	

c. Teacher reviews expository text structure by comparing and contrasting with narrative texts.	
d. Teacher gives book talks on the five informational texts to be used in next series of CALCs: *African Beginnings*, *The African Slave Trade*, *Exploration Into Africa*, *Great Zimbabwe*, *Ancient Africa*.	
4. CALC groups select an informational text to read and discuss.	5 minutes
Friday:	
1. Students read informational books selected on Thursday. Fill in Wondering As We Read form.	30 minutes
2. CALCs meet and discuss book, then brainstorm issues for next CALC.	25 minutes
3. Teacher works with whole class to discuss discrepancies between informational texts, textbook, and novels.	30 minutes
4. Students write in learning logs about their new thinking about Africa.	15 minutes
5. Teacher initiates discussion about research projects for next two weeks.	25 minutes
a. KWL chart	
b. CALC group members work individually on a research question from the region they have been studying: cultural, geographical, historical focus.	
6. CALCs meet to discuss individual questions and how to complement one other's research.	10 minutes
Week Four: Research Projects & CALCs Support	
Monday:	
1. Students share research questions with class and discuss what type of sources they will need and use.	35 minutes
a. Teacher reviews bibliography format.	
b. Students brainstorm how to make notes.	
2. CALCs meet to discuss issues from informational books read on Friday.	30 minutes
3. Teacher revisits Rubric for Content Area Literature Circle and asks students to critique their discussions on the Self-Evaluation forms.	25 minutes
4. Students begin research with books, teacher or library resources, and Internet and write in learning logs.	35 minutes

5. Students share their needs, new questions, and research conundrums with class.	10 minutes
Tuesday–Thursday:	
Research is interspersed with teacher mini-lessons and reviews on finding sources, paraphrasing, meeting in CALCs for support and discussion.	
Friday:	
1. Movie: *Portrait of Africa*	
2. Students keep notes of interest	
3. Class discussion on movie: connections, feelings, interest	
Week Five: Research Project & Presentation	
Monday:	
1. CALCs meet to discuss research projects and connections between projects.	20 minutes
2. Teacher gives review of presentations: format, audience, points of interest.	30 minutes
3. CALCs meet to discuss presentation for Friday.	20 minutes
4. Individual students continue research.	45 minutes
5. Teacher asks CALCs to share presentation ideas with whole group.	20 minutes
Tuesday–Thursday:	
Students finish individual research and plan a presentation with their CALC. Teacher supports with mini-lessons.	
Friday:	
1. CALCs present research.	90 minutes
2. CALCs meet once more to discuss their process as a group. Individuals fill in Self-Evaluation forms.	30 minutes
3. Teacher wraps up unit with briefing on how the process went, what worked, what could be improved.	15 minutes

References
and Resources

Adler, D. (1994). *A picture book of Sojourner Truth*. New York: Holiday House.

Adler, D. A. (1997). *Lou Gehrig: The luckiest man*. New York: Harcourt.

Allen, J. (1999). *Words, words, words: Teaching vocabulary in grades 4–12*. York, ME: Stenhouse.

Altman, S., Lechner, S., & Perrone, D. (2002). *Ancient Africa: Modern rhymes for ancient times*. Danbury, CT: Children's Press.

Alvermann, D., Dillon, D., & O'Brien, D. (1987). *Using discussion to promote reading comprehension*. Newark, DE: International Reading Association.

Angelou, M. (2003). *Kofi and his magic*. New York: Crown Books.

Arnold, N. (1998a). *Blood, bones, and body bits* (T. De Saulles, Illus.). London: Scholastic.

Arnold, N. (1998b). *Disgusting digestion* (T. De Saulles, Illus.). New York: Scholastic.

Atkin, B. (1993). *Voices from the fields: Children of migrant farm workers tell their stories*. New York: Scholastic.

Atwell, N. (1998). *In the middle: New understanding about writing, reading, and learning* (2nd ed). Portsmouth, NH: Heinemann.

Bamford, R. A., & Kristo, J. V. (Eds.). (1998). *Making facts come alive: Choosing quality nonfiction literature K–8*. Norwood, MA: Christopher-Gordon.

Barnes, D., & Todd, F. (1995). *Communication and learning revisited*. Portsmouth, NH: Heinemann.

Bartoletti, S. (2001). *Black potatoes: The story of the Great Irish Famine, 1845–1850*. Boston: Houghton Mifflin.

Bash, B. (1990). *Tree of life: World of the African baobab*. Boston: Little, Brown.

Beach, R. (1993). *A teacher's introduction to reader-response theories*. Urbana, IL: National Council of Teachers of English.

Beane, J. A. (1997). *Curriculum integration: Designing the core of democratic education*. New York: Teachers College Press.

Beasant, P. (1992). *1000 facts about space*. New York: Scholastic.

Bendick, J., Levin, M., & Simon, L. (1972). *Mathematics illustrated dictionary: Facts, figures, and people including the new math*. New York: McGraw-Hill.

Benedict, S., & Carlisle, L. (Eds.). (1992). *Beyond words: Picture books for older readers and writers*. Portsmouth, NH: Heinemann.

Berger, M. (1995). *Discovering Jupiter: An amazing collision in space*. New York: Scholastic.

Berger, M. (2000). *Scholastic science dictionary*. (H. Bonner, Illus.). New York: Scholastic.

Berger, M., & Berger, G. (1998). *Why don't haircuts hurt? Questions and answers about the human body*. New York: Scholastic.

Berger, M., & Berger, G. (1999a). *Do stars have points? Questions and answers about stars and planets* (V. Di Fate, Illus.). New York: Scholastic.

Berger, M., & Berger, G. (1999b). *How do flies walk upside down? Questions and answers about insects*. New York: Scholastic.

Berger, M., & Berger, G. (2000). *Can you hear a shout in space? Questions and answers about space exploration* (V. Di Fate, Illus.). New York: Scholastic.

Bessire, M. (1999). *Great Zimbabwe*. London, UK: Watts.

Biesele, M., Elusbe, B. O., & Royal, K. (1997). *San (Heritage Library of African Peoples, South Africa)*. New York: Rosen.

Borden, L., & Kroeger, M. K. (2001). *Fly high!: The story of Bessie Coleman*. New York: McElderry Books.

Bowser, J. (1993). Structuring the middle-level classroom for spoken language. *English Journal 82* (1), pp. 38–41.

Branley, F. M. (1998). *Planets in our solar system*. New York: HarperTrophy.

Bridges, L. (1995). *Assessment for continuous learning*. Los Angeles: Galef Institute.

Brinkley, E. H. (1999). *Caught off guard: Teachers rethinking censorship and controversy*. Boston: Allyn & Bacon.

Brooks, J., & Brooks, M. (1993). *In search of understanding: The case for constructivist classrooms*. Alexandria, VA: Association for Supervision and Curriculum Development.

Brooks, P. G. (1995). *Cleopatra: Goddess of Egypt, enemy of Rome*. New York: HarperCollins.

Bruchac, J. (2000). *Sacajawea*. New York: Scholastic.

Buehl, D. (2001). *Classroom strategies for interactive learning* (2nd ed.). Newark, DE: International Reading Association.

Bulion, L. (2002). *Fatuma's new cloth*. Kingston, RI: Moon Mountain.

Bunting, E. (1994). *A day's work*. New York: Clarion Books.

Bunting, E. (1998). *So far from the sea*. New York: Clarion Books.

Burns, M. (1975). *The I Hate Mathematics! Book* (M. Weston, Illus.). New York: Scholastic.

Clark, D. (2000). *South Africa: The culture*. Bellevue, WA: Turtleback Press.

Claybourne, A., Doherty, G., & Treays, R. (2000). *Usborne encyclopedia of planet earth*. New York: Scholastic.

Cole, S. (1985). *When the tide is low*. New York: HarperCollins.

Coleman, E. (1998). *The riches of Osceola McCarty*. Morton Grove, IL: Whitman.

Comber, B., & Simpson, A. (Eds.). (2001). *Negotiating critical literacies in classrooms*. Mahwah, NJ: Erlbaum.

Cooper, J. (1995). The role of narrative and dialogue in constructivist leadership. In L. Lambert, D. Walker, D. Zimmerman, J. Cooper, M. Lambert, M. Gardner, & P. J. Slack, (Eds.), *The constructivist leader* (pp. 121–133). New York: Teachers College Press.

Cowcher, H. (1990). *Antarctica*. Manchester, UK: Futech.

Crane, C. (2001). *L is for lone star: A Texas alphabet*. Chelsea, MI: Sleeping Bear Press.

Crowdog, M. (1990). *Lakota woman*. New York: HarperCollins.

Cummings, D. (2003). *The Nile: Great rivers of the world*. Cleveland, OH: World Almanac Library.

Curtis, N., & Allaby, M. (1993). *Planet earth*. Boston: Houghton Mifflin.

Daniels, H. (2002). *Literature circles: Voice and choice in book clubs and reading groups* (2nd ed.). Portland, ME: Stenhouse.

Davis, K. (2001). *Don't know much about the solar system*. New York: HarperCollins.

Demi. (1997). *One grain of rice*. New York: Scholastic.

Dewey, J. (1916). *Democracy in education*. New York: Macmillan.

Dewey, J. (1933). *How we think*. Boston: Heath.

Dewey, J. (1938). *Experience in education*. New York: Macmillan.

Dingle, D. T. (1998). *First in the field: Baseball hero Jackie Robinson*. New York: Hyperion.

Dyson, M. J. (1999). *Space station science: Life in free fall*. New York: Scholastic.

Enzensberger, H. M. (1997). *The math devil: A mathematical adventure*. New York: Holt.

Farmer, N. (1998). *A girl named Disaster*. New York: Puffin Books.

Feinberg, J. R. (1992). *Reading the sports page: A guide to understanding sports statistics*. New York: Silver Burdett Press.

Fennessey, S. M. (2000). *History in the spotlight: Creative drama and theatre practices for the social studies classroom*. Portsmouth, NH: Heinemann.

Ferreira, A. (2002). *Zulu dog*. New York: Foster Books.

Flint, A. S., Campbell, D., & Halderman, K. (1999). *Literature circles: A professional's guide*. Westminister, CA: Teacher Created Materials.

Florian, D. (1998). *Insectlopedia*. New York: Scholastic.

Frager, A. (1993). Affective dimensions of content area reading. *Journal of Reading, 36* (8), 616–622.

Freedman, L. (1993). Teacher talk: The role of the teacher in literature discussion groups. In K. M. Pierce & C. J. Gilles (Eds.), *Cycles off meaning: Exploring the potential of talk in learning communities* (pp. 219–235). Portsmouth, NH: Heinemann.

Freedman, L. (1996). *Once upon a time: Storying in a middle school classroom.* Unpublished dissertation, University of Arizona, Tucson.

Freedman, R. (1999). *Babe Didrikson Zaharias: The making of a champion.* New York: Clarion Books.

Freeman, E. B., & Person, D. G. (1998). *Connecting informational children's books with content area learning.* Boston: Allyn & Bacon.

Gallardo, E. (1993). *Among the orangutans: The Birute Galdikas story.* San Francisco: Chronicle Books.

Gardner, H. (1993). *Multiple intelligences: The theory in practice.* New York: Basic Books.

Gates, P. (1995). *Wild technology: Inventions inspired by nature.* London: Kingfisher.

Gee, J. P. (1996). *Social linguistics and literacies* (2nd ed.). Bristol, PA: Taylor & Francis.

Getz, D. (2000). *Purple death: The mysterious flu of 1918.* New York: Holt.

Gibbons, G. (1999). *Stargazer.* New York: Holiday House.

Golding, V. (1998). *Traditions from Africa.* Chicago, IL: Raintree.

Goodman, D. (1999). *The reading detective club: Solving the mysteries of reading.* Portsmouth, NH: Heinemann.

Govenar, A. (2000). *Osceola: Memories of a sharecropper's daughter.* New York: Hyperion Books.

Graham, I. (1991). *Looking at space.* Glendale, CA: Action.

Green, J. (1998). *Race to the moon: The story of Apollo 11.* London: Watts.

Gregorowski, C. (2000). *Fly, eagle, fly: An African tale.* New York: McElderry Books.

Grifalconi, A. (1986). *The village of round and square houses.* Boston: Little, Brown.

Grifalconi, A. (2002). *The village that vanished.* New York: Dial Books.

Guiberson, B. (1993). *Cactus Hotel.* Logan, IA: Perfection Learning.

Guiberson, B. (2000). *Into the sea.* New York: Holt.

Gustafson, J. (1994). *Voyager: An adventure through space.* Bellevue, WA: Turtleback Books.

Harrison, M., & Stuart-Clark, C. (1989). *Peace and war: A collection of poems.* Oxford, UK: Oxford University Press.

Harste, J. (1994). Literacy as curricular conversations about knowledge, inquiry, and morality. In R. Ruddell, M. Ruddell, & H. Singer (Eds.), *Theoretical models and processes of reading,* (4th ed., pp. 1220–1242). Newark, DE: International Reading Association.

Harvey, S. (1998). *Nonfiction matters: Reading, writing, and research in grades 3–8.* York, ME: Stenhouse.

Harvey, S., & Goudvis, A. (2000). *Strategies that work: Teaching comprehension to enhance understanding.* York, ME: Stenhouse.

Haskins, J. (1998). *African beginnings.* New York: HarperCollins.

Haskins, J., & Benson, K. (2001). *Building a new land: African Americans in colonial America.* New York: HarperCollins.

Hehner, B. (1999). *First on the moon: What it was like when man landed on the moon.* Toronto, Ontario, Canada: Hyperion/Madison Press.

Hetfield, J. (2000). *The Yoruba of West Africa.* New York: Powerkids Press.

Hetfield, J., & Johnston, M. (2003). *The Masaai of East Africa: Celebrating the peoples and civilizations of Africa.* New York: Powerkids Press.

Hoose, P. (1993). *It's our world, too! Young people who are making a difference: How they do it—How you can, too.* New York: Farrar, Straus & Giroux.

Hoose, P. (2001). *We were there, too! Young people in U.S. history.* New York: Farrar, Straus & Giroux.

Ibazebo, I. (2000). *Explorations into Africa.* New York: Silver Burdett.

Ivey, G. (1999). A multicase study in the middle school: Complexities among young adolescent readers. *Reading Research Quarterly, 34* (2), 172–192.

Jackson, D. M. (1996). *The bone detectives: How forensic anthropologists solve crimes and uncover mysteries of the dead.* Boston: Little, Brown.

Jimenez, F. (1997). *The circuit: Stories from the life of a migrant child.* New York: Scholastic.

Johnson, H. (2000). "To stand up and say something": "Girls only" literature circles at the middle level. *The New Advocate, 13* (4), 375–388.

Johnson, H., & Freedman, L. (2001). Talking about content knowledge at the middle level: Using informational trade books in content-area literature circles. *The Language and Literacy Spectrum, 11,* 52–61.

Johnston, P. (1992). Coming full circle: As teachers become researchers so goes the curriculum. In N. A. Branscombe, D. Goswami, & J. Schwartz, (Eds.), *Students teaching, students learning* (pp. 66–95). Portsmouth, NH: Boynton/Cook–Heinemann.

Jones, R. (1976). *The acorn people.* New York: Dell Books.

Jones, T. D., & English, J. A. (1996). *Mission earth: Voyage to the home planet.* New York: Scholastic Press.

Kaiser, S. (1994). *Exploring cultural identity: Creating an environment that invites cultural connections through a family studies inquiry and children's literature.* Unpublished master's thesis, University of Arizona, Tucson.

Keene, E. O., & Zimmerman, S. (1997). *Mosaic of thought: Teaching comprehension in a reader's workshop.* Portsmouth, NH: Heinemann.

Kenda, M., & Williams, P. S. (1995). *Math wizardry for kids: Solve puzzles, play games, have fun! Surprise yourself with your own wizardry.* New York: Barrons Juvenile.

Kessler, C. (2000). *No condition is permanent.* New York: Philomel Books.

Kessler, C. (2002). *My great-grandmother's gourd.* New York: Orchard Books.

King, M. L., Jr. (1997). *I have a dream: An illustrated edition.* New York: Scholastic Press.

Knight, M. B., Melnicove, M., & O'Brien, A. B. (2002). *Africa is not a country.* Brookfield, CT: Millbrook Press.

Kracht, James. (2003). *World explorer: People, places, and cultures.* Needham, MA: Prentice-Hall.

Kurtz, J. (1998). *The storyteller's beads.* San Diego, CA: Gulliver Books.

Lambert, D. (1997). *The Kingfisher young people's book of oceans.* London: Larousse Kingfisher Chambers.

Lambert, L. (1995). Introduction. In L. Lambert, D. Walker, D. Zimmerman, J. Cooper, M. Lambert, M. Gardner, & P. J. Slack (Eds.), *The constructivist leader,* pp. xi–xv. New York: Teachers College Press.

Lasky, K. (1994). *The librarian who measured the earth.* Boston: Little, Brown.

Lauber, P. (1994). *Fur, feathers, & flippers: How animals live where they do.* New York: Scholastic.

Leedy, L. (1993). *Postcards from Pluto: A tour of the solar system.* New York: Scholastic.

Lehr, S. (Ed.). (1995). *Battling dragons: Issues and controversy in children's literature.* Portsmouth, NH: Heinemann.

Lerner, M., & McMullen, D. (2002). *Math smart junior: Math you'll understand.* Minneapolis, MN: Sagebrush.

Lewin, T. (1998). *The storytellers.* New York: HarperCollins

Lewis, J. P. (2000). *Freedom like sunlight: Praisesongs for Black Americans.* Mankato, MN: Creative Editions.

Lindfors, J. W. (1999). *Children's inquiry: Using language to make sense of the world.* New York: Teachers College Press.

Lipka, J., & McCarty, T. (1994). Changing the culture of schooling: Navajo and Yup'ik cases. *Anthropology & Education Quarterly, 25,* 266–284.

Loewen, J. W. (1995). *Lies my teacher told me: Everything your American history textbook got wrong.* New York: New Press.

Long, B. (1997). *Jim Thorpe: Legendary athlete.* Springfield, NJ: Enslow.

Longfellow, H. W. (2001). *The midnight ride of Paul Revere.* Brooklyn, NY: Handprint Books.

Low, R. (2003). *Peoples of the desert.* New York: Powerkids Press.

Lowenstein, D. (1976). *Graphs.* London: Watts.

Lunardini, C. (1997). *What every American should know about women's history.* Holbrook, MA: Adams.

Lyman, F. (1987). Think Trix Matrix. Alexandria, VA: ASCD.

Lyman, F. (2001). *Inside the Dzanga-Sangha rain forest: Exploring the heart of Central Africa.* New York: Workman.

MacCauley, D., with Ardley, N. (1998). *The new way things work: From levers to lasers, windmills to Web sites, a visual guide to the world of machines.* Boston: Houghton Mifflin.

MacLeod, E. (2003). *Albert Einstein: A life of genius.* Toronto, Ontario, Canada: Kids Can Press.

Mallery, A. L. (2000). *Creating a catalyst for thinking: The integrated curriculum.* Boston: Allyn & Bacon.

Manzo, A. (1969). The ReQuest procedure. *Journal of Reading, 11,* 123–126.

Markle, S. (1997). *Discussing graph secrets: Experiments, puzzles, and games exploring graphs.* New York: Atheneum.

McAnally, K. (1995). *Letters from the Canyon: An alphabetical visit to the Grand Canyon.* Flagstaff, AZ: Grand Canyon Association.

McBrier, P. (2001). *Beatrice's goat.* New York: Antheneum.

McIntire, S. (2001). *American Heritage Book of great American speeches for young people*. Indianapolis, IN: Wiley.

McKissack, P., & McKissack, F. (1999). *Black hands, white sails: The story of African American whalers*. New York: Scholastic.

Meier, D. (2002). *The power of their ideas: Lessons from a small school in Harlem*. Boston: Beacon Press.

Meltzer, M. (2001). *There comes a time: The struggle for civil rights*. New York: Scholastic.

Merrick, P. (2000). *Morocco (Countries, faces, and places)*. Toronto, Ontario, Canada: Child's World.

Merrill, J., & Palmer, J. (1999). *Toothpaste millionaire*. New York: Houghton Mifflin.

Miles, L., & Smith, A. (1998). *The Usborne complete book of astronomy and space*. New York: Scholastic.

Miller, M. (1999). *Words that built a nation: A young person's collection of historic American documents*. New York: Scholastic Press.

Mitton, J., & Mitton, S. (1998). *Scholastic encyclopedia of space*. New York: Scholastic.

Mollel, M. (1995). *The orphan boy*. New York: Houghton Mifflin.

Mollel, M. (1999). *My rows and piles of coins*. New York: Clarion Books.

Mooney, M. E. (2001). *Text forms and features: A resource for intentional teaching*. Katonah, NY: Owen.

Mora, P. (2002). *Maria paints the hills*. Minneapolis, MN: Sagebrush.

Morley, J., Bergin, M., & James, J. (2001). *An Egyptian pyramid*. New York: Bedrich Books.

Morris, M. (1992). *Katherine and the garbage dump*. Toronto, Ontario, Canada: Second Story Press.

Moscovitch, A. (2000). *Egypt: The people*. New York: Crabtree.

Moss, J. (1997). *Bone poems*. New York: Workman.

Muirden, J. (1993). *Stars and planets*. New York: Scholastic.

Murphy, J. (1990). *The boys' war: Confederate and Union soldiers talk about the Civil War*. New York: Clarion Books.

Murray, J., & Sheehan, S. (2003). *Africa: A cultural atlas for young people*. New York: Facts on File.

Myers, W. D. (2001). *The greatest: Muhammad Ali*. New York: Scholastic.

Nelson, M. (2001). *Carver: A life in poems*. New York: Scholastic.

Nerburn, K., & Menglekoch, L. (1991). *Native American wisdom*. San Rafael, CA: New World Library.

Neuschwander, C. (2003). *Sir Cumference and the sword in the cone*. Watertown, MA: Charlesbridge.

Newman, S. (2000). *The African slave trade*. Bellevue, WA: Turtleback.

Ogle, D. (1986). K-W-L: A teaching model that develops active reading of expository text. *The Reading Teacher, 39,* 564–570.

Onyefulu, I. (1997). *A is for Africa*. New York: Puffin.

Opitz, M. F., & Rasinski, T. V. (1998). *Good-bye round robin: 25 effective oral reading strategies*. Portsmouth, NH: Heinemann.

Pappas, T. (1993). *Fractals, googols, and other mathematical tales*. New York: WideWorld.

Park, F., & Park, G. (1998). *My freedom trip: A child's escape from North Korea*. Honesdale, PA: Boyds Mills Press.

Parker, D., Engfer, L., & Conrow, R. (1998). *Stolen dreams: Portraits of working children*. Minneapolis, MN: Lerner.

Parker, S., & West, D. (1993). *Brain surgery for beginners and other major operations for minors*. New York: Scholastic.

Parry, F. (1995). *Day of Ahmed's secret*. New York: HarperTrophy.

Patent, D.H. (1999). *Flashy, fantastic rain forest frogs*. New York: Walker.

Paulsen, G. (1988). *Hatchet*. New York: Atheneum.

Perry, D. (2001). *Yakabou must choose*. West Conshohocken, PA: Infinity.

Peterson, R., & Eeds, M. (1990). *Grand conversations: Literature groups in action*. Toronto, Ontario, Canada: Scholastic.

Pierce, K. M. (Ed.). (2000). *Adventuring with books: A booklist for Pre-K–Grade 6*. Urbana, IL: National Council of Teachers of English.

Pringle, L. (2000). *The environmental movement: From its roots to the challenges of a new century*. New York: HarperCollins.

Quinlan, S. E. (2003). *The case of the monkeys that fell from the trees*. Honesdale, PA: HHBoyds Mills Press.

Quintana, A. (1999). *The baboon king*. New York: Laurel-Leaf Books.

Raphael, T. (1986). Teaching question answer relationships, revisited. *The Reading Teacher, 39*, 516–522.

Reutzel, D., & Cooter, R., Jr. (1996). *Teaching children to read: From basals to books*. Englewood Cliffs, NJ: Prentice-Hall.

Rhodes, L., & Shanklin, N. (1993). *Windows into literacy: Assessing learners K–8*. Portsmouth, NH: Heinemann.

Regan, C., & Cremin, B. (1997). *Africa (Continents)*. Chicago, IL: Raintree.

Robertson, J. F., & Rane-Szostak, D. (1996). Using dialogue to develop critical thinking skills: A practical approach. *Journal of Adolescent and Adult Literacy, 39* (7), 552–556.

Rochman, H. (1988). *Somehow tenderness survives: Stories of Southern Africa*. New York: HarperTrophy.

Rockwell, A. (2000*). Only passing through: The story of Sojourner Truth*. New York: Knopf.

Roe, B., Stoodt, B., & Burns, P. (2001). *The content areas: Secondary school literacy instruction* (7th ed.). New York: Houghton Mifflin.

Rogers, B. R., & Rogers, S. D. (2002). *Zimbabwe: Enchantment of the world series*. Dublin, Ireland: Children's Press.

Rosenberg, A. (2003). *Nigeria: The culture*. New York: Crabtree.

Rosenblatt, L. (1978). *The reader, the text, the poem*. Carbondale, IL: Southern Illinois University Press.

Rosenblatt, L. M. (1983). Literature as exploration (4th ed.). New York: Modern Language Association.

Ruiz, R. (1991). The empowerment of language-minority students. In C. Sleeter (Ed.), *Empowerment through multicultural education* (pp. 217–227). Albany, NY: State University of New York Press.

St. Antoine, S. (2003). *American prairie, the Gulf coast, the North Atlantic coast*. Minneapolis, MN: Milkweed.

Sarbin, T. (1986). *Narrative psychology: The storied nature of human conduct*. Westport, CT: Praeger.

Sayre, A. (2000). *If you should hear a honey guide*. New York: Houghton Mifflin.

Scieszka, J., & Smith, L. (1995). *Math curse*. New York: Viking.

Scott, E. (1998). *Close encounters: Exploring the universe with the Hubble space telescope*. Burbank, CA: Disney Press.

Shapiro, L. (1987). *A book of days in American history*. New York: Scribner.

Short, K., Harste, J., & Burke, C. (1996). *Creating classrooms for authors and inquirers*. Portsmouth, NH: Heinemann.

Short, K., & Pierce, K. M. (Eds.). (1990). *Talking about books: Creating literate communities*. Portsmouth, NH: Heinemann.

Simon, S. (1985). *Saturn*. New York: HarperCollins.

Simon, S. (1987). *Mars*. New York: Mulberry Books.

Simon, S. (1988). *Volcanoes*. New York: Morrow Junior Books.

Simon, S. (1992). *Mercury*. New York: HarperCollins.

Simon, S. (1993). *Wolves*. New York: HarperCollins.

Simon, S. (1996). *The heart: Our circulatory system*. New York: Scholastic.

Simon, S. (1997a). *The brain: Our nervous system*. New York: Scholastic.

Simon, S. (1997b). *Neptune*. New York: HarperTrophy.

Simon, S. (1998a). *Bones: Our skeletal system*. New York: Scholastic.

Simon, S. (1998b). Comets, meteors, asteroids. New York: HarperTrophy.

Simon, S. (1998c). *Jupiter*. New York: HarperCollins.

Simon, S. (1998d). *Muscles: Our muscular system*. New York: Scholastic.

Simon, S. (1999). *Venus*. Minneapolis, MN: Sagebrush.

Simon, S. (2000). *The universe*. New York: Scholastic.

Smith, F. (1988). *Joining the literacy club: Further essays into education*. Portsmouth, NH: Heinemann.

Smith, F. (1998). *The book of learning and forgetting*. New York: Teachers College Press.

Smith, F. D. (2003). *Elsie's war: A story of courage in Nazi Germany*. London: Lincoln.

Smith, K. (1994). *New paths to power: American women 1890–1920*. New York: Oxford University Press.

Spangenburg, R., & Moser, K. (2001). *A look at Mars*. Minneapolis, MN: Sagebrush.

Springer, J. (1997). *Listen to us: The world's working children*. Berkeley, CA: Publisher's Group West.

Stanley, D. (1994). *Shaka: King of Zulus*. Carmel, CA: Brown.

Stanley, J. (1992). *Children of the Dust Bowl: The true story of the school at Weedpatch camp*. New York: Trumpet Club.

Steele, P. (1995). *Black holes and other space phenomena*. New York: Scholastic.

Stock, C. (2001). *Gugu's house*. New York: Clarion Books.

Swartz, D. (1998). *G is for googol: A math alphabet book.* Berkeley, CA: Tricycle Press.

Swinburne, S., & Brandenburg, J. (2001). *Once a wolf.* New York: Sandpiper.

Tames, R. (2001). *The end of apartheid: A new South Africa.* Portmouth, NH: Heinemann.

Tchana, K. (2002). *Sense pass king: A story from Cameroon.* New York: Holiday House.

Thimmesh, C. (2000). *Girls think of everything: Stories of ingenious inventions by women.* Boston: Houghton Mifflin.

Tierney, R. J., & Readence J. E. (2000). *Reading strategies and practices: A compendium* (5th ed.). Boston: Allyn & Bacon.

Totten, S., Johnson, C., Morrow, L. R., & Sills-Briegel, T. (Eds.). (1999). *Practicing what we preach: Preparing middle level educators.* New York: Falmer Press.

Trumble, K. (1999). *Cat mummies.* New York: Clarion.

Tsuchiya, Y. (1988). *Faithful elephants: A true story of animals, people, and war.* Boston: Houghton Mifflin.

Valencia, S. W. (1998). *Literacy portfolios in action.* Fort Worth, TX: Harcourt Brace.

Volavkova, H. (1993). *I never saw another butterfly: Children's drawings and poems from Terezin concentration camp, 1942–1944.* New York: Schocken Books.

Vorderman, C. (1996). *How math works: 100 ways parents and kids can share the wonders of mathematics.* New York: Readers Digest.

Vieira, L. (1994). *The ever-living tree: The life and times of a coast redwood.* New York: Walker.

Vygotsky, L. (1978). *Mind in society.* Cambridge, MA: Harvard University Press.

Walker, D., & Lambert, L. (1995). Learning and leader theory: A century in the making. In L. Lambert, D. Walker, D. Zimmerman, J. Cooper, M. Lambert, M. Gardner, & P. J. Slack (Eds.), *The constructivist leader* (pp. 1–27). New York: Teachers College Press.

Walker, R. (2001). *Body: Bones, muscle, blood and other body bits.* New York: DK.

Washington, B. T. (2000). *Up from slavery.* (W. L. Andrews, Ed.). Oxford, UK: Oxford Unversity Press.

Weintraub, A. (2003). *The Sahara desert: The biggest desert.* New York: Powerkids Press.

Wertsch, J. (1981). The concept of activity in Soviet psychology. Armonk, NY: Sharpe.

West, D. (1992). *53½ things that changed the world and some that didn't.* New York: Scholastic.

Whitin, P., & Whitin, D. J. (2000). *Math is language too: Talking and writing in the mathematics classroom.* Urbana, IL: National Council of Teachers of English.

Wick, W. (1997). *A drop of water: A book of science and wonder.* New York: Scholastic.

Wiese, J. (1997). *Cosmic science.* Indianapolis, IN: Wiley.

Wilde, S. (2000). *Miscue analysis made easy: Building on student strengths.* Portsmouth, NH: Heinemann

Wilhelm, J. D. (1996). *Standards in practice: Grades 6–8.* Urbana, IL: National Council of Teachers of English.

Wilhelm, J. D. (1997). *"You gotta be the book": Teaching engaged and reflective reading with adolescents.* New York: Teachers College Press.

Williams, K. (1991). *Galimoto.* New York: HarperTrophy.

Wolk, R. (2002). Tragic flaws. *Education Week* [Online]. Available at: www.edweek.org.

Wood, J. (1990). *Caves.* New York: Scholastic.

Wood, K. D., & Dickinson, T. S. (Eds.). (2000). *Promoting literacy in grades 4–9: A handbook for teachers and administrators.* Boston: Allyn & Bacon.

Wood, L. (2001). *Skeletons.* New York: Scholastic.

Yopp, R. H., & Yopp, H. K. (2001). *Literature-based reading activities* (3rd ed.). Boston: Allyn & Bacon.

Zemelman, S., Daniels, H., & Hyde, A. (1998). *Best practice: New standards for teaching and learning in America's schools* (2nd ed.). Portsmouth, NH: Heinemann.

Zemser, A. (2000). *Beyond the mango tree.* Minneapolis, MN: Sagebrush.

Websites for Middle Level Educators

Math

Forum
mathforum.org/dr.math/drmath.middle.html
mathforum.org/midpow/

NCTM
http://my.nctm.org/eresources/journal_home.asp?journal_id=3

David Rock (problems-solutions)
www.olemiss.edu/mathed/middle/

Missouri math project
www.coe.missouri.edu/~mathed/M3/

MMAP
mmap.wested.org/

Archaeology

www.usd.edu/anth/midarch.htm

Physical education

PE Central
http://pe.central.vt.edu/lessonideas/pelessonplans.html

John L. Hubisz
www.psrc-online.org/curriculum/book.html

Astronomy

darkskyinstitute.org/astronomy.html

Curriculum (history)

Crossroads (Full history)
www.askeric.org/Virtual/Lessons/crossroads/sec4/

Sociology and psychology

Donn (activities and lesson plans)
http://members.aol.com/Donnpages//Sociology.html

English language arts

Young adult literature
http://falcon.jmu.edu/~ramseyil/yalit.htm

Art lessons (jr. high)

homepage.mac.com/krohrer/iad/lessons/middle/middlelessors.html

Science

http://www.middleschoolscience.com/

Web ring logo
www.geocities.com/damselflywings/

Cohasset (whales)
www.ssec.org/idis/cohasset/TblCnt.htm

Interdisciplinary

Cohasset
www.ssec.org/idis/cohasset/chs.htm

Lessons

www.eecs.umich.edu/mathscience/funexperiments/agesubject/
middleschool.html

Fractals
Math.rice.edu/~lanius/frac

Teacher.Net (Lesson bank)
http:// www.teachers.net/cgi-bin/lessons/sort.cgi?searchterm=middle

Teacher.Net
http://www.teachers.net/lessons/search.html

Donn (lesson ideas)
http://members.aol.com/Donnpages//Ideas.html

Teacherszone.com
http://www.teacherszone.com/

Lesson plans

Donn (across curriculum)
http://members.aol.com/Donnpages//LessonPlans.html
http://members.aol.com/Donnpages//2LessonPlans.html
http://members.aol.com/Donnpages//3LessonPlans.html
http://members.aol.com/Donnpages//4LessonPlans.html

Kathy Schrock
http://school.discovery.com/lessonplans/index.html

EdScope, L.L.C
http://www.lessonplanspage.com/

Edmund Sass (Ed. Resources and lesson plans)
http://www.cloudnet.com/~edrbsass/edres.htm

Collection in various curricula areas
henson.austin.apple.com/edres/mslessons/ms-menu.shtml

Web portal for educators

Teach-nology
http://www.teach-nology.com/

Library

Linda: Virtual library
www.sldirectory.com/stetson.html

Magazine

Midlink, NC
www.cs.ucf.edu/~midLink/

Critical evaluation of a Web site
Kathy Schrock
School.discovery.com/schrockguide/evalmidd.html

Diaries, teacher guide

Report
www.middleweb.com

Teacher guide
www.middleweb.com/1stDResources.html

Miscellaneous

Cybrary
www.geocities.com/Athens/Academy/6617/

Judy Horn
http://www.middleschool.net/

Education-world
www.education-world.com/search/

National Middle School Association
http://www.nmsa.org/

ASCD
www.middleschool.net

APMS
www.strato.net/~apms/

Index

About the Authors

Lauren Freedman is currently an Associate Professor in the Department of Teaching, Learning, and Leadership at Western Michigan University. Her current research interests include inquiry and the use of multiple materials across the curriculum; integrated curriculum at the middle level; teacher preparation in literacy education with an emphasis on middle level and secondary; and issues of diversity and multiculturalism in teacher preparation. She received her Ph. D. in Language, Reading, and Culture from University of Arizona, Tucson.

Holly Johnson is an Associate Professor at the University of Cincinnati, where she coordinates the Middle Childhood Education Program and teaches courses in literacy and children's/adolescent literature. Prior to her position in higher education, Holly taught middle level language arts/social studies in Kentucky and in Arizona. She also taught middle level mathematics and industrial arts in Botswana, Africa as a Peace Corps volunteer. Her current interests focus on the use of adolescent literature and children's picture books for exploring issues of social justice. She has published papers in numerous journals and has published another Christopher Gordon text with Lauren Freedman entitled *Inquiry, Literacy, & Learning in the Middle Grades*.